Mentoring

Mentoring

A Strategic Approach for
Business Development

Lesly Jules

To order additional copies of this book, contact:
Xlibris Corporation
1-888-795-4274
www.Xlibris.com
Orders@Xlibris.com
50897

CONTENTS

ACKNOWLEDGEMENTS

I am indebted to my wife, Kerline Toussaint, who supported me in the journey of producing this book. Her enduring and genuine patience has proven to be helpful in many situations.

My sincere appreciation should also be extended to my mentor, Jean-Pierre Bal, for his constant and endless personalized support and encouragement.

I am grateful to James Lachaud, Christie Laratte, Kristin Boers and Carol & Richard Mears who have devoted the time in reviewing the book content.

INTRODUCTION

Small businesses are notorious when it comes to job and wealth creation. It is agreed that those two elements are important for economic growth in most world-class economies. Their meaning in developing countries is even greater. But it is not always the case that small businesses would meet these expectations because of constraints of all kinds. It is the understanding of this reality that has prompted the implementation of Business Development Service programs worldwide. Some of these programs focus their attention on the transmission of entrepreneurial and management skills which are capable to effectively empower small business leaders in the marketplace. The means by which this transmission happens is a business mentor.

A mentoring relationship exemplifying this exists between Hugo Philemy and Ralph Edmond. Hugo met Ralph through a humanitarian agency that he was sponsoring. Hugo has been in contact with that agency to get a loan to expand his business in selling honey. Hugo would get his fresh honey in the countryside and bring it to the city where the market is.

He would collect empty ketchup bottles and fill them with his honey. Yet, the bottle would smell like ketchup even with the honey inside. This was not a very good combination. He would then put a black and white label of which content is hardly readable, except for the word: HONEY. As Ralph is in the pharmaceutical industry, he knows most of the plastic bottle suppliers. Initially, he thought that he would simply recommend Hugo to one of them. But it would take more than pointing to a supplier to help Hugo out, and Ralph knew that.

The first things they did were setting a place where they would meet, setting a time to meet on a regular basis, developing an agenda and making sure that the expectations and responsibilities were clear and agreed upon between both parties. Second, they started "bench-marking" around by studying the competition and the industry. Both of them had the opportunity to really see if they could compete or not in this venture. They saw they could. But in order to add value to the product, they built a plan about how they will address matters such as accounting, marketing and production

Initially, they would meet at Ralph's company. Hugo would go out to collect the information they need. Then they would analyze the data and see how they could use them in the honey business. Ralph would introduce Hugo to financial suppliers and help him understand the cash flow principles. Ralph would also introduce him to other business people for networking.

In the end, Hugo was able to demonstrate his capacity to develop new products, including marketing and cost analysis. Then, Hugo had a highly competitive product in comparison to imported honey. Hugo developed entrepreneurship and leadership skills that ensured the growth and sustainability of his company. But the best thing that happened to Hugo is that, like Ralph, he became a mentor himself to a less experienced business person. Ralph not only assisted Hugo in developing his business but he also guided him to develop of leaders within other people.

Skills development in entrepreneurship and management is a must for entrepreneurs who have to compete in an ever-changing environment. And mentoring, as it is based on experiential learning, is one of the mediums by which those skills can be acquired. That was the premise or the philosophy upon which business mentoring programs were implemented. It is suggested that skills in the areas of planning, product development, marketing, human resource management and finance are necessary for entrepreneurs to succeed in their venture. In fact, the capacity of a small business to meet the expectations of a given economy is based, most of the time, on the entrepreneurial and management skills of the business leaders. While a lack of those skills can negatively affect the enterprise, they can be developed through an experiential learning program with the support of a mentor like Ralph and Hugo.

Many studies consider mentoring as an effective tool to promote business and leadership development, but mentoring programs are not always apt at delivering the outcomes at the expected level. The purpose of this book is to reflect on how a mentoring program is to be structured so that it contributes to the effectiveness of small business leaders both in the area of personal and organizational development thus influencing their profitability in the marketplace. It is the intention of this book to bring new understanding and insights into the conceptual and empirical framework of strategic mentoring in regards to entrepreneurial or leadership competency development.

Mentoring is in fact an opportunity offered to small business leaders to set and work on developmental goals they may have for their personal and organizational life. And it allows entrepreneurs to develop hands-on competencies and provides them with resources that are adapted or tailored to their needs and challenges. Nevertheless, this book discloses as well that strategic mentoring program, in order to be effective, needs to be carefully designed and implemented intelligently.

A mentoring program not only has to be clear with what it intends to accomplish, but also it has to be able to strategically and effectively target its participants, namely the program coordinator, the mentors and the mentees. The survival and effectiveness of the program largely depends on the accuracy of the choices and the support that is provided to the mentors and mentees during the implementation phase of the program. In so doing, training and orientation sessions to the participants is a must while the program will make sure that the relationships between the parties are properly nurtured. Finally, an environment has to be created where feedback is expressed and documented and also the program needs to develop evaluation tools to ensure its continual refinement as well as its effectiveness. All of this implies that effective facilitated mentoring programs do not just happen. Their success is more a matter of careful design, planning and implementation than mere luck and this is exactly what this book wants to highlight in its three chapters.

The first one consists of a literature review and an overview of the conceptual framework regarding small businesses. Thus, it explores the characteristics and specificities of small businesses. The latter faces all kinds of administrative, operating and strategic constraints. Those constraints are investigated in a detailed manner. Finally, an assessment is conducted in terms of the leadership and/or entrepreneurship competencies that are needed for a small business leader to be effective and ensure the profitability of the company in the marketplace.

The second chapter introduces the mentoring concept as an effective business development services approach. Thus it covers its origin, the various avenues and format that a mentoring program may espouse. Finally, is presented a set of mentoring programs assessed by their commonalities and differences. A set of key success factors is derived from the identified differences and commonalities. The third chapter focuses on those key success factors. In so doing, it addresses the foundation, the strategies and the structures and systems that are conducive to the design of an effective strategic mentoring program.

It is our hope that the recommendations provided in this book are taken into consideration, not only by the scholars and practitioners who are involved in the field of strategic mentoring, but also serves the decision-makers who are interested in small business development. This book will hopefully serve as a guideline that helps bring clarification to the importance and usefulness of leadership or entrepreneurial competency development. Such competency acquired through strategic mentoring is likely to positively influence the profitability of the small businesses. Since strategic mentoring is considered a valid option, this book offers a set of key success factors and a framework that can serve as a pathway to foster the successful and intelligent implementation of a mentoring program.

Chapter I

Small business specificities

Although small businesses pose a serious problem of definition, they are recognized by many as a vector of economic development. They are considered as a reliable source of wealth creation. They are also perceived as one of the best tools for social integration by their capacity to generate productive employment. However, they face constraints of all kinds that can hinder the free expression of their potential. It is important that those constraints be addressed. More importantly, small business leaders have to identify the capacities or competencies that are needed for them to be effective in an ever-changing environment. First, let us consider what the small business definition entails.

a. What is in a name?

Economists are very careful when it comes to defining the small business concept, especially in the globalization context. This concept is best approached through pre-defined indicators or characteristics such as size, sales turnover, industry, management structure, etc. Those elements may vary from one region to another and from one country to another. A classification is made of the concept in the high income and in the low income countries for a more accurate definition. However, even among Western countries small businesses are difficult to define and the definitions provided are not always the same:

The Official Journal of European Union adopts the following definitions: *"An enterprise is considered to be any entity engaged in an economic activity, irrespective of its legal form. This includes, in particular, self-employed persons and family businesses engaged in craft or other activities, and partnerships or associations regularly engaged in an economic activity."* And the small business assessed by staff headcount and financial ceilings, is defined as: *"an enterprise which employs fewer than 50 persons and whose annual turnover and/or annual balance sheet total does not exceed EUR 10 million."* More specifically, in terms of headcount, the Recommendation Commission adopts the following nomenclature:

- micro firm: 0-9 employees
- small firm: 10-49 employees
- medium firm: 50-249
- employees large firm: over 250 employees

If defining a small business in the European context is simple, it is apparently one of the most difficult tasks in the United States of America. In fact, the United States Office of Small Business Administration (SBA) currently uses various sets of criteria which range from programs regulation to industry. Finally, a definition for the concept was expressed and it takes into account the number of employees and the annual sales.

However, the definition presented by Professor Scott Holmes and Brian Gibson has been accepted by the Small Business Coalition (SBC) which settled the debate over the definition of small business in America. The definition is the following: *"A small business is a business which is independently owned and operated, with close control over operations and decisions held by the owners. Business equity is not publicly traded and business financing is personally guaranteed by the owners. The business will have less than twenty employees.*" It is obvious that the definitions represent the small business both in qualitative and quantitative terms. We will retain the aspects of the definitions such as size, operation facility, market and management in this study.

b. Constraints faced by small business leaders

If indeed the economy can rely on the contribution of small businesses in the area of job and wealth creation, it is not automatic that small businesses live up to that standard. Sometimes, they are incapacitated by weaknesses inherent to their leaders, and the same reality exists everywhere in the world.

It happens that small businesses do not bring about the expected results for many reasons. A major reason is found in the internal weakness in most small businesses which affect negatively their chances of success as well as their life expectancy. Among the weaknesses of small business leaders, one notices a lack of leadership, management and entrepreneurial skills which are critical to the success of a business venture. Most of the constraints faced by small business leaders rest in the way they conduct their businesses or their behavior that lacks entrepreneurial spirit to succeed in their undertaking.

Vesper suggests that skills in the areas of planning, product development, marketing, human resource management, finance and marketing are necessary for entrepreneurs to succeed in their venture. In fact, beside the market feasibility and the intrinsic motivation of the entrepreneur, the capacity of a small business to meet the expectations of a given economy is also based on the entrepreneurial and management skills of the business leaders. Lack of those skills can negatively affect the enterprise.

Chrisman and Leslie argue that most of the small business leaders' weaknesses can be categorized into administrative, operating and strategic problems. This classification is what we use in this paper in order to provide a global view of the situation of the small businesses.

The administrative issues regroup items such as organizational structure, personnel, accounting and licensing. They can be described as follows:

- **Building an effective organizational structure**. Small business leaders do not often design an organizational chart and use it as a basis for decision making. It is very likely for them to contract apprentices who will become employees at some stage. Sometimes, the hiring process does not imply the outlining of a comprehensive job description and that latter makes evaluation and performance review a painful process. It goes without saying that it affects the productivity of these companies as well as the motivation and the remuneration of the personnel. The lack of preparation and ignorance of the promoter towards the requirements of management and business operations is deplorable. That is also valid for the application of business ethics principles which are concerned with the respect of laws and regulations such as work ethics.

- **Maintaining regular bookkeeping and calculation of cost and price**. The level of informality of the small businesses combined with the lack of management knowledge from their leaders have a major influence on how they manage their finances. To begin with, some are not able to make the crucial difference between sales turnover and profit. This implies that regular bookkeeping needs to be done and that costs are calculated and monitored continuously. This way of doing business weakens the capacity of the company to be competitive in the market place.

- **Adopting procedures to formalize their business operations vis-à-vis the government.** It is to the advantage of a small company to formalize its operations. It allows it to have access to a license of operations that is a requirement for the opening of a corporate bank account. Without this license, they are neither able to advertise their products nor attract customers beyond their immediate location.

Operating issues include production, operations structure, and marketing. They can be described as follow:

- **Assessing and putting in place an adequate production structure.** Most small enterprises are born in the household of the owner. An increase in activities will prompt the owner to move to another facility and hire more staff, but the technology or production process remains the same while not fully taking into account the production need. Knowing the process roughly, the business owner, based on his experience as a workman or a simple craftsman, launches the business operations with simple and antiquated materials which can poorly provide the basic functions of the activity envisaged. For example, a business that produces banana flour will use a peanut butter mill to crush the raw material.

Indeed, it will work initially but it does not have the potential to take the business to the next level, like increasing the capacity to serve a broader market or lower production cost.

Risks exist in this type of company. Serious accidents often occurred, yet only a few incidents are reported to the government office in charge of that. In addition, the business-operations are not always conducted under good conditions and often they do not meet the requirements and expectations of the consumers. Moreover, the raw materials and the inputs used are often of bad quality; sometimes the promoter buys the inputs cheaply or recovers leftovers from larger companies, to use as inputs. This way of doing things compromises the expected quality and keeps potential customers at bay. The latter hold a negative image about local products which reinforces the "made-in effect" where customers choose products based on origins.

- **Conducting a market survey prior to production.** Small business owners are usually people who are very good at something, namely in the combination of different skills to create a value-added product. Some have been working previously in similar companies to the ones they currently manage, where they acquired the know-how. Based on the mastery of certain skills, they then decide to go into business. They make a product (or offer a service) and try to market it to people located, most of the time, in their immediate environment. The idea of getting feedback from previously identified or potential customers is not always on their agenda. In that case, they end up with a number of products that are difficult to market.

The strategic segment is composed of items such as business planning, feasibility studies and strategic planning. The present study which focuses mostly on the strategic issues, describes them as follow:

-   **Gathering information on customers' satisfaction and competition strategies.** When the small business owners sell to customers, their attitude is driven much more by the money they get for their goods and services at this specific moment in time instead of developing a relationship with the latter. It is very uncommon for them to keep track of customers' satisfaction. By the same token, it is not considered valuable to collect information from their competitors to improve the quality of their products and services. The phenomenon of imitation worsens this situation, since many individuals will launch the same products, thus increasing the number of competitors. In the end, the buyer is unable to differentiate between products and ends up buying from the seller who is nearest to his center of activity.

-   **Writing a business plan and negotiating with bankers.** The idea of planning the future of the business is not part of some small business leaders' behavior. This condition prevents them from having an accurate assessment of their strengths and weaknesses as well as those of their competitors. It also prevents them from anticipating constraints and opportunities related to their ventures. This is a possible explanation for the stagnation and death of some small businesses. They are caught in a daily management that does not allow them to envision the future and take advantage of it. That could mean going for another market, developing a new line of products, recruiting more competent employees, developing alliances with other small businesses and so on.

- **Investigating the possibility to serve a foreign market** (regional or international). Most of the small businesses only consider their city as a potential area of business. They are not accustomed to surveying other markets at a regional or international level even when Information Communication Technologies (ICTs) allows them to do so at a relatively low cost. That would help them to expand their operations, increase their profit and become more competitive.

The problems listed above need attention from the small business leaders. If they are not addressed, the effectiveness and success of small businesses can be seriously impaired.

c. Necessary leadership competencies for small business leaders

Luthans, Stajkovic & Ibrayeva argued that the establishment of entrepreneurial training, if executed successfully, can lead to an increase of entrepreneurial self-efficacy in transitional economies. Then, there is an opportunity to strengthen the capacity of small business leaders by providing to them opportunities to minimize their weaknesses while building on their strengths so that they can play a significant role in the economy. Among the leadership competencies that are necessary for small business leaders to cultivate, one can cite the following:

o Ability to communicate and develop a vision for the company
o Ability to network with other entrepreneurs

o Ability to empower coach and lead employees
o Ability to undertake or participate in community or
   social initiatives
o Ability to adopt and practice sound business ethics and
   principles
o Ability to cultivate continual learning
o Ability to cultivate effective customer relationships
o Ability to plan, organize and manage work and life in a
   balanced way
o Ability to take calculated risks

The above abilities can be described as follows:

- **Ability to develop and communicate a vision for the
   company.** In Alice in Wonderland, Lewis Carroll reminds
   us that:" *If you don't know where you want to go, just about
   any path will lead you there.*" Unfortunately, this is the case
   for some small business leaders who get caught in the
   daily management of their business operations without
   having in mind a sense of direction about where they
   are heading.

   It is a must for any business leader to cast a vision
   about where he/she wants to go; because more than
   anything it allows one to prioritize among the various
   necessary tasks to make a business work. John Maxwell
   says that: "*A person who has a dream knows what he is
   willing to* give up *in order to* go up." In other words, a
   vision allows one to act strategically. That competency
   is a must for any company that strives to be competitive
   in the marketplace. In his book, Built to Last, Jim
   Collins, considers visioning as the main distinguishing
   characteristic of the most enduring and successful
   corporations. Kouses and Posner assert that:" *The leader's*

clarity of purpose and ability to articulate both the vision and shared values give certainty and purpose to others who may be unsure, who are afraid, or who would otherwise have difficulty achieving greatness on their own."

The vision can be represented in the business plan document which contextualizes where the company is going, what it will do to get there, what are the elements (stakeholders, etc.) in its environment that need to be taken into account and what progress is to be monitored, when and at which level. However, as the business plan emphasizes the human resources that need to be mobilized to work toward the vision, it is necessary that the latter be communicated to the people involved so that it is effectively implemented.

Peter Drucker reminds us that: *"The distinction that marks a plan capable of producing results is the commitment of key people to work on specific tasks. Unless such commitment is made, there are only promises and hopes, but no plan."* The ability to conceive a vision is therefore as important as communicating it which is the first step to create ownership. In the same vein, Warren Bennis and Joan Goldsmith argue that: *"Leaders articulate and define what had previously remained implicit or unsaid; then they invent images, metaphors, and models that provide a focus for attention. By so doing, they consolidate or challenge prevailing wisdom. In short, an essential factor in leadership is the ability to influence and create meaning for the members in the organization."*

- **Ability to network with other entrepreneurs**. As the world is becoming more a global village, a key competitive advantage for a company, and especially a small one, is to focus itself on its core competency while outsourcing other business functions to third parties in a win-win strategy. Logistics outsourcing implies that any company can excel only in some activities or competencies related to its value chain to guarantee its success; it is the trade of the company. In an article entitled Outsourcing Integration from Juyne Linger published in Harvard Business Review, logistics outsourcing is represented as a key concept in management because it increases competitiveness and offers greater operational flexibility. The nature of competition evolves in a fast way; it would be impossible for a company to compete with others in isolation. It is now the involvement of team work or a network.

The companies must work together to sustain their activity in an ever-changing business environment. The companies as they focus themselves on their key competencies they can rely on those of their partners, reinforcing at the same time and to a significant degree their value chain and their competitive advantage, which they could not carry out in isolation. If one important business objective is to increase the margins, it is important that the company concentrates on core activities which can at the same time increase the incomes and reduce the costs, which Fahey and Randall call the "strategic push". According to Steve Kaplan, *"One of the most common and most effective methods of growing with minimum investment and risk is through strategic alliances. Strategic alliances give your business the opportunity to grow by providing more products and services to more customers than you can offer on your own."*

As some small business leaders do not learn to partner with other business leaders, most of the time they cannot develop that critical size or mass that is needed to compete with large corporation and even to address the needs of a foreign market. John Maxwell posits that: "*Working together increases the odds of winning together.*" So for a small business leader, two things are important. On the one hand it is necessary to develop a body of knowledge of value chain and, on the other hand, to cultivate the good habit or the value of collaborating with other small business leaders. Peter Singe, cited by Cloke and Goldsmith observed that "*Everyone knows that no work ever gets done by following rules. It gets done through the informal networks.*"

- **Ability to empower, coach and lead employees**. John Craig, cited by Maxwell & Dorman argues that:" *No matter how much work you can do, no matter how engaging your personality may be, you will not advance far in business if you cannot work through others.*" In fact, as mentioned above one individual alone cannot achieve the vision of the organization; therefore, it is necessary that those who will participate in the implementation of the vision not only understand it, buy in to it, own it but also be properly coached and empowered in so doing. Indeed, one of the responsibilities of a leader is to assist others around him/her in developing their leadership potential.

In his book entitled The 360° Leader, John Maxwell argues that: "*Most people do not discover their strengths on their own. They often get drawn in the daily routine and simply get busy. They rarely explore their strengths or reflect on their successes or failures. That is why it is so valuable for them to have a leader who is genuinely interested in helping them recognize their strengths.*" This can take place by identifying strengths and development areas, formulating plans to address those and channeling people in areas where they can add value to every organizational function (value chain) based on their talents. In this context, Jay Conger and Beth Benjamin posit that it is important to hold an individualized transformation leadership position by treating each subordinate as an individual and serve as coaches and teachers through delegation and meaningful learning opportunities.

Delegation at this stage implies that trust exists between the small business leader and his/her subordinates and consequently this means that either he or she has created an environment conducive to learning and where the employees are safe to give and receive feedback. It also means that the employees are being delegated responsibilities (for their work) progressively based on their capacity which is monitored along with the agreed upon goals. Some small business leaders have a hard time delegating responsibilities and power or build a team around them.

Some small business leaders are inclined to say that:" *To get this done the way it should be, I have to do it myself.*" With such a mentality, very few leadership tasks (goal setting and decision making, e.g.) are delegated to employees. And that behavior affects considerably the performance of both employees and the company. Peter Drucker asserted that: "*The person who always knows exactly what other people cannot do, but never sees anything they can do, will undermine the spirit of her organization.*"

- **Ability to undertake or participate in community or social initiatives.** The main objective of any business ought to be to ensure that it is profitable. There is no objection to that. But objecting that a business can be socially responsible is what the Economist Milton Friedman aimed at in his article entitled: "The Social Responsibility of Business is to Increase its Profit." According to the author: *"The political principle that underlies the market mechanism is unanimity. In an ideal free market resting on private property, no individual can coerce any other, all cooperation is voluntary, all parties to such cooperation benefit or they need not participate. There are no values, no "social" responsibilities in any sense other than the shared values and responsibilities of individuals. Society is a collection of individuals and of the various groups they voluntarily form."*

In this article Friedman was concerned about CEOs and their responsibility vis-à-vis their shareholders. However, for this current paper the focus is rather on business owners vis-à-vis the environment or the context where the business operation is taking place. It is not the purpose of this paper to nurture the debate over the concept of Corporate Social Responsibility but rather to emphasize that the actions of a business leader can go beyond just the goal of making money. Newsman Tom Brokaw, cited by John Maxwell, observed that:" *It is easy to make a buck. It is a lot tougher to make a difference."*

As the small business leader develops business acumen and meets a need of a growing market it can be useful for him/her to broaden his/her scope of influence beyond the marketplace to the community or society at large. In so doing, the participation in community or social initiatives can take multiple forms namely that of advocating for environmental issues, playing the role of a mentor on behalf of a less experience person, financially supporting charity causes, taking part in community projects, etc. In so doing, the small business leader participates in something bigger than he/she and enriches his/her life in the process of enriching other people's lives. There is no cause greater than striving, acting and living for a better world.

- **Ability to adopt and practice sound business ethics.** In the process of creating a better world, it is crucial that the business leader cultivate the practice of business ethics principles beyond just posting the company's mission and values statement on the wall so that visitors can see it for the sake of reputation. Charles Muchene, the Kenya Country Leader of Price Waterhouse Coopers, brilliantly expresses his concerns about business ethics as follow: *"It is perhaps not an unfair comment to say that the standards of societal and business ethics in our region have continued to be eroded over the years. We have seen a "casino economy" mentality emerge that focuses almost entirely on short-term gains, at whatever cost. We continue to uphold as heroes those who have been involved in unethical acts. Our children are growing up in an environment where the dividing line between right and wrong is very grey. Regrettably, the tried and tested values of hard work and decency have been lost to many. Can we recapture them? Is it possible for us to focus on developing long-term success based on sound ethical principles?*

  The answer is that we must, if we expect our businesses to survive in the long run for the benefit of its stakeholders. And this is not a far-fetched assertion. We have over the last two or so years seen European buyers of such products as tea, flowers, fruits and vegetables subjecting their East African suppliers, as well as those from other parts of the world, to rigorous ethical audits. Why? Because there is a growing demand by their customers and other stakeholders to shy away from those businesses that may be engaged in unethical behavior, we can only expect this trend to expand to other groups and regions.

Leadership is all about—taking the risk of going where others fear to tread, in the firm conviction that it is the right thing to do and will pay off in the future. And as many CEOs in East Africa told us, it is that courage and leadership that earns ethical businesses and their CEOs the respect of their peers."

The reality described by Muchene is no different from that of small businesses in most countries. That is why ethical values are important in the leadership competency repertoire of the small business leader and also can be considered as a wining behavior in business, especially in the long run. Robert Sternberg put it this way:" *Values mediate how one balances interests and responses, and collectively contribute even to how one defines a common good."* The practice of business ethics takes into account, the working environment, licensing or patenting, declaration revenues and paying taxes, etc.

In a general sense, practicing business ethics is about portraying how the business ought to relate with all the stakeholders involved, namely the shareholders, the employees, the customers, the government and society at large. It is true in all life, not just in business, that it is impossible to exercise authentic leadership without integrity. Like in the case of the corporate social responsibility, business ethics enable the business leader to understand the opportunity to make a difference, the role and the responsibility he/she holds vis-à-vis the rest of the world. John Maxwell puts it this way: "The *entire population of the world—with one minor exception—is composed of others."*

- **Ability to cultivate continual learning.** Because they excel at producing a particular product, some business leaders assume that they have mastered it all or they know all there is to know. However, it is important for a leader to define what he/she needs to learn (and also unlearn) to keep abreast of the key success factors related to the success of the organization as well as for self-efficacy. Doing that implies nurturing a sense of continual learning especially so, when the very principles that work today might not tomorrow. This learning is not only about business development but also about one-self through reflection on one's experience. It is said that our greatest strength can also be our greatest weakness. Therefore a sense of awareness or consciousness is necessary to assess what needs to be learned in our fast changing environment.

Edwards and Usher assert that: "*Learning is the condition of flexibility, and flexibility is seen as the condition of learning. In a risk society, one cannot stop learning, not only in relation to work but also in relation to life more generally. Thus, lifelong learning becomes integral to the discourses and practices of business.*" Warren Bennis considers that curiosity and daring are to be regarded as basic ingredients of leadership. He said:" *The leader wonders about everything, wants to learn as much as he can, is willing to take risks, experiment, try new things. He does not worry about failure, but embraces errors, knowing he will learn from them.*"

Such a way of seeing and doing things requires truly that the leader undergo an unlearning process in order to learn other behaviors that are conducive to learning especially that of self-reflection, willingness to change, openness to feedback and active listening. Addressing the issue of listening, Goldsmith and Bennis raise the question: *"How do we learn to listen to what we do not know, or does not fit, or we do not want to hear? To start with, we recognize that it is exactly these communications that have the ability to wake us up, set us free, allow us to learn something new, and release us from patterned thinking. Trivial, ordinary, acceptable conversations do not change us."*

- **Ability to cultivate effective customer relationships.** There is no company without customers. Peter Drucker argues that:" *Who is the customer? is the first and crucial question in defining the purpose and business mission. It is not an easy, let alone and obvious question. How it is being answered determines, in large measure, how the business defines itself."* The answer to that question determines also the type, the nature and the depth of the relationship that will be pursued with the customers. Some small business leaders take their customers for granted assuming that they will always be there. Consequently they fail to continuously add value to their products/services as well as cultivating a genuine relationship with them. This tendency is complicated with the fact that small businesses do not always conduct market research or bench-mark their competitors to better position themselves.

According to Kotler & Dubois, the cost of retaining a customer is five times inferior to that of prospecting a new customer. A defensive marketing approach is less costly than an offensive one for which it is necessary to confront directly the competition. Therefore, it is necessary for them, cost wise, to know their customers and cultivate a winning relationship with them. While there is a variety of strategies to retain customers, it can be as simple as adopting the right behavior. Simple winning behaviors can consist of collecting feedback from customers' satisfaction on a regular basis; anticipating customers' needs; spending time with them when they stop at the business; getting to know and calling them by their names; saying thank you and have a nice day; showing empathy and being diligent. All these can be summed up by acting proactively instead of reactively by trying to satisfy disappointed customers or wondering why they do not show up or while sales went down, etc. According to Carl Albrecht, the company should be designed in a way that allows it to create and deliver the kinds of value the customer seeks.

- **Ability to plan, organize and manage work and life in a balanced way.** Unlike the above behaviors, this one is the most difficult for business leaders to adopt. Yet, it is an important aspect that can greatly influence a leader's both personal and organizational development. At the personal level, such leaders experience a sense of loneliness that is not healthy as it increases the level of stress which impairs their performance. Collin Hastings reported that: "*Many work extraordinarily long hours, driven by the desire to succeed. Even when they have the glamorous trappings of success, most find that there is still something missing. They mention the absence of close enduring personal friendships; regret at having missed out on their children's growing up; fears about their physical health; and, above all, that recurring sense of loneliness. Such feelings afflict executives in large and small organisations alike. The problem is compounded because these people cannot admit to themselves, never mind others, that they experience loneliness and uncertainty, and sometimes doubt whether the sacrifices of the job are balanced by the benefits.*"

The question of work-life balance is important for leaders to address, especially the small business leaders. Some of them at the early beginning of their companies could not afford the appropriate staff that they wanted. As a response, they had to get involved in every detail regarding business operations. Unfortunately, this way of handling business sooner became a habit even when the company reaches cruise speed or a certain level of maturity. Regarding the issue of work-life balance, Jack Welch said that: "*Today, no CEO or company can ignore it.*" So it is an issue that needs to be dealt with at the utmost. And even when most people consider it is easier said than done, the remedy to the work-life issue is called, discipline. Maybe, at the beginning, it is important for small business leaders to come with a definition of success or a definition of vision that incorporates every aspect of their life (family, health, leisure or hobby, etc.) and not just the financial.

- **Ability to take calculated risks**. In portraying a leader, Warren Bennis said:" *A leader is, by definition, an innovator. He does things other people haven't done or don't do. He does things in advance of other people. He makes new things. He makes old things new.*" Such an understanding of a leader certainly puts the concepts of innovation and risk-taking at the center of his/her activities. That is precisely the reason why entrepreneurship and leadership are often associated to one another. In fact, Joseph Schumpeter, cited by Meier & Baldwin, consider innovation and risk-taking as basic entrepreneurial functions which constitute in essence the fundamental characteristics of entrepreneurs.

Indeed, there is no growth or progress without risk and it happens that the leader is the only one convinced of the necessity to take the risk to make things happen. Henry David Thoreau, cited by N.T. Perkins, said that:" *The one who does nothing runs as much risks as the one who undertakes a venture.*" Risk in the context of a small business leader might have to do with launching a new line of products, targeting a new market, investing in the promotion of a new venture or reengineering the whole business operation, etc. If in reality some people are risk averse, it is necessary for any body who consider him/herself a small business leader to learn how to assess and take calculated risk in proper time. There is a very narrow distance between visioning and risk-taking. Leaders are people who have the capacity to cope with uncertainty and ambiguity as they define the reality or the desired future. But, such behaviors also imply the possibility of making mistakes and learn from them.

The above abilities are important qualities for a small business leader to add to his/her leadership competency repertoire. If nurtured and utilized, such leadership competency is likely to enhance the personal effectiveness of the small business leaders as they enrich the local economy through job and wealth creation.

CHAPTER II

SMALL BUSINESS DEVELOPMENT

SERVICES

Based on the role small businesses play in a given economy, it is important for their needs or constraints to be addressed. In that context, some small business development initiatives with the objective of assisting small business leaders to develop entrepreneurial and management skills to perform better in the market place while creating jobs and wealth in the economy is a must. These programs are more effective when offered via mentors. Those latter can be professional consultants and entrepreneurs from medium and large established businesses who are willing to volunteer in mentoring programs. This chapter covers the origin of mentoring as well as the various avenues and format it may espouse. All business mentoring programs aims at one thing: Business Development. But as the programs differ in their approach, the assessment of their commonalities and differences is likely to facilitate the identification of key success factors.

a. The strategic mentoring approach

Skills development in entrepreneurship and management is a must for entrepreneurs who have to compete in an ever changing environment. And mentoring, as it is based on experiential learning, is one of the mediums by which those skills can be acquired. That was the premise or the philosophy upon which business mentoring programs were implemented. Vesper suggests that skills in the areas of planning, product development, marketing, human resource management and finance are necessary for entrepreneurs to succeed in their venture. In fact, the capacity of a small business to meet the expectations of a given economy is based, most of the time, on the entrepreneurial and management skills of the business leaders. While a lack of those skills can negatively affect the enterprise, they can be developed through an experiential learning program with the support of a mentor.

Citing a study conducted by the Gallup organization, Kenneth Cloke and Joan Goldsmith reported some dramatic improvements in the Air Force as a result of the introduction of a strategic mentoring program. The study revealed that 81.9 percent of those being mentored received above average or excellent performance evaluations after completing the mentoring process, compared with only 40.9 percent before. Self-confidence in regards to promotion increased from 63.6 percent to 90.9 percent afterward, and decision-making ability improved to 81.9 percent from 72.7 percent before.

Murray stated that mentoring has the potential to bridge the gap between skills required for business and leadership effectiveness and the skills taught in traditional business school. She puts it in perspective by saying that: "*four of the skills that are most often neglected in school curricula-decisiveness, tolerance of uncertainty, resistance to stress, and use of personal power—are particularly appropriate for modeling and coaching by a skillful mentor.*" Joel Makower argued that business mentoring can provide significant benefits for companies as it helps in reducing operating costs, early identification of liabilities and risks, enhancement of competencies, etc. Thus, a variety of business mentoring models is being implemented in different parts of the world. It is important to compare some of those models in search for common key success factors.

b. Origins of the mentoring concept

Rooted in the Latin, the term "mentor" means "who develops the mind." Most literature on mentoring identifies the origin of the concept in Greek mythology. Homer's epic poem, The Odyssey, traces the Greek evolution of the concept as follows:

The Odyssey is, in part, the story of one man's adventures after the Trojan War. After the successful sack of Troy, Odysseus embarked with several ships and many followers to return to his native Ithaca, off the western coast of the Peloponnesian peninsula. In what should have been a fairly standard trip-there was the usual side trip to sack and pillage 'Lauchachia' en route just to keep certain that standard operating procedures honed by years of planning and manoeuvres remained in good order—Odysseus incurred the wrath of Poseidon, the god of earth and sea. Despite Odysseus's efforts to meet his goal on time and within budget, events beyond his control intervened. Instead of a few weeks, Odysseus was gone for 10 more years.

During this time, his wife, Penelope, steadfastly remained loyal to him. Although pursued by several dozen suitors from all over the Greek world, she remained virtuous. She also was faced with some budgetary difficulties. In the manner of the times, the suitors who wanted to replace Odysseus in Penelope's bed as well as lay claim to Odysseus's kingdom hung around the palace drinking and feasting-at Penelope's expense. This drain on Ithaca's coffers did not escape the gods. Athena, in particular, took pity on Penelope and successfully argued that the gods should allow Odysseus to return. As part of her plan, she told Telemachus, Odysseus's son, who was a baby when Odysseus went off to war but who was now full grown, to outfit a ship and go looking for his father.

Fed up with the actions of the suitors, who had virtually taken over his father's palace, Telemachus embarked on what he felt would be an impossible mission. He was helped in this effort by the man Odysseus left behind to look after the palace and grounds, Mentor. Athena assumed Mentor's appearance and accompanied Telemachus on the journey. Along the way, "Mentor" gave him encouragement—the encouragement that he needed to develop into a fully functioning, responsible adult. Telemachus was relieved to be doing something. He was a man of action even though he perceived that the odds were against him.

Like all good mentors, Athena imbued Telemachus with a sense of responsibility. In seeking to master his challenging assignment, Telemachus discovered his inner strength. The babbling teenager became an articulate, courageous adult who impressed others with his leadership potential. With his mentor's help and support, Telemachus gained confidence and achieved a degree of success that he had not previously thought possible. In short, under a mentor's guidance, Telemachus showed leadership qualities similar to those his father had displayed during the Trojan War.

Apparently, the mentor refers to someone with certain skills and abilities who accompany a less experienced person in the journey of self-mastery or professional development. Based on Homer's epic poem and Les Aventures de Telemaque from Francois Fenelon, a French mystic, religious writer and educator, Caruthers, cited by Roberts pictured the mentor as: "*a father figure, a teacher, a role model, an approachable counselor, a trusted adviser, a challenger, an encourager.*"

Those characteristics which explain the role of the mentor and the mentoring phenomenon can be also traced to the craft guilds which started in the Middle-Ages. Murray argued about how these societies used mentoring in order to structure the professions of merchant, lawyer, goldsmith, and more. The model then was the one of a master who would take a young man to his care as a "protégé". The young man would, under the master's guidance, develop skills inherent to the professions until he became a master himself and would run the shop at the old master's death or retirement. It was an acceptable path of succession planning. Later on, the master-apprentice relationship evolved to a more complex or formal one of an employer-employee in contemporary societies.

Cloke and Goldsmith arguing about the importance of a mentor put it this way: "*Very simply, strategic mentors encourage us to wake up and craft a carefully planned approach to purposeful self-development. By sharing their experience, discernment, and insight, they increase our capacity to learn. They show us how to cultivate awareness and authenticity in ourselves and others. They do so by allowing a part of what they discovered and who they became to be passed on, through us, to future generation*".

Arguing about the benefits of mentoring, the Harvard Business Essentials on Coaching and Mentoring acknowledges that mentoring helps to transfer important tacit knowledge from one person to another. It continues by saying: "*Tacit knowledge is knowledge that is difficult to codify and store in written or database form. It is the type of knowledge that is found in people's heads and nowhere else . . . mentoring provides a channel for transferring tacit knowledge from one generation of employees to another, or from highly experienced managers to those with les experience. In the absence of this channel, important information is isolated.*"

Today, mentoring is becoming a very common practice in capacity development. Mentoring opportunities are being sought in various fields: psychology, higher education, government, business, adult education, management and organizational behavior, leadership, etc. And each field has its own appreciation of the terms mentor and mentoring. But in essence, mentoring refers to a process where a more experienced person develops a relationship with a less experienced person to promote experiential learning for personal and/or professional development. And mentoring relationships can espouse different forms and avenues.

c. The avenues of mentoring

According to Bauer, a mentoring relationship can be categorized as: 1) grooming mentoring where a mentor is working one-on-one with a specific mentee or protégé and 2) networking-mentoring where several mentors in different capacities work with one mentee or more mentees. Mentoring sessions can take many different forms depending on the context of both parties in a mentoring relationship. Consequently, different mentoring arrangements including one-on-one mentoring, business group to business group mentoring, and more formalized training (one mentor sharing their knowledge with a group of entrepreneurs) are in use.

When similar training needs are identified for a group of entrepreneurs involved in mentoring relationships, group mentoring and sector training opportunities can be developed to meet these needs. Common requests for this type of group mentoring include: export assistance, financial skills, market development, food processing, non-traditional crop production, and ISO standards.

In essence, mentoring can be informal or formal and internal or external.

- **Informal mentoring.** As the first expression of mentoring is traced in Homer's epic poem therefore, mentoring relationships initially were informal. Informal mentoring refers to the fact that a mentor may have assisted a mentee in career advancement or guided the latter through the pathways of a profession without an organizational structure that helped establish the outcomes of the relationships. In that case, a certain chemistry or natural attraction is expected to be found between the parties in a relationship that is more emotional rather than instrumental. And such relationship occurs spontaneously. Sullivan, cited by Audet and Couteret, argued on the relevancy of matching compatible people in a mentoring relationship, stating that: "*since the chemistry that needs to be established between two people is so important, all pre-selection attempt or imposed matching of a mentor and a mentee is doomed to failure.*"

- **Formal mentoring.** Although Murray admits that the chemistry of many informal mentoring relationships cannot be created through structure, she nevertheless argued that formal mentoring can be as beneficial to today's mentees as it was for the apprentices in medieval times. She commented that: "*assisting, guiding, and controlling the mentoring process have proven to be feasible in both historical and modern times.*" Formal mentoring refers, in fact, to a mentoring program designed to facilitate a relationship between a mentor and a mentee through a structure which helps in the definition of learning objectives and acceptable behaviors expressed in a formal contract between the parties involved in the mentoring relationship. This book is concerned with this particular type of mentoring.

- **Internal mentoring**. A large number of the mentoring programs occur inside a given organization. In that case, both the mentor and mentee belong to the same organization. A mentor can be assigned to a mentee (formal mentoring) or a mentee may look for a mentor on his own (informal mentoring). The objective is for the mentee who aspires to more responsibilities in leadership at the organization to be accompanied by a more experienced person in the organization to develop skills suited for the business environment. In this type of mentoring, the mentor, because of his/her proximity to the mentee can be more available to the latter for hands-on consultation. This type of mentoring is reputed to be more successful when it happens across branches as it reduces liabilities such as internal competition and its corollaries.

- **External mentoring**. In contrast to the internal mentoring program, the mentor and mentees in the external mentoring are not necessarily involving in the same organization as employees or employer. This type of mentoring, operating as a host program, may imply the recruitment of mentors and mentees. Most of the time, the relationship between those latter is facilitated by the support of a third party, namely a program coordinator. Obviously, this type of mentoring requires a certain level of formality since the coordinator will have the responsibility to screen mentors and mentees, match them together, train them, structure the relationship and monitor the progress made in regards to pre-defined outcomes.

Independent of the aforementioned typology, mentoring can espouse various formats. The ones that are most commonly used are:

- **One-on-one mentoring**, also called face to face mentoring, implies a relationship where two people are present—a mentor and a mentee. In this format, through the mentoring relationship the developmental need of the mentee is able to be addressed specifically in a tailored manner. Each mentee is supposedly facing different issues or opportunities and they are addressed individually. While this format allows a precise monitoring of outcomes, it consumes however an important amount of resources. But this format is considered by far the most effective means of capacity development.

- **Group mentoring** also called a mentoring circle can be explained as a relationship between one mentor and a group of mentees or a group of mentors and one mentee. The mentoring program which adopts the one-to-many version is able to categorize the issues faced by different participants and address them accordingly. The one constraint in this format is that individual specific needs which do not fall into a certain category might remain unaddressed. The other version, namely the many-to-one, offers the opportunity to the mentee to benefit from different mentors in various identified developmental areas. In this context, one function that is not addressed by one particular mentor is likely to be addressed by another. The key is the availability of those mentors.

- **Network mentoring** usually happens in association settings where each member of the association has a certain expertise that can be beneficial to the other members. Each one is then invited to share experiences and knowledge or when there is a need to address. The diversity of the industries where the members belong can sometimes pose a problem of relevancy of the information to be shared. However, members having similar interests in the organization can organize a peer-to-peer mentoring initiative.

- **Cyber-mentoring**. It is possible to cite e-mentoring or cyber-mentoring in this list of mentoring formats. In fact, this format unlike the others is dependant upon communication and information technologies (ICT) such as e-mail, chat rooms, websites, phones, etc. If at the beginning some people were skeptical vis-à-vis the effectiveness of such format, Single and Single, cited by Hanford, reported that recent research revealed that e-mentoring confers the same benefits to mentees as face-to-face relationships.

d. Commonalities and differences in mentoring programs

Various types of mentoring programs are operating using the formats mentioned above. Their objective is mainly to foster learning and behavioral change. The commonalities they share reveal the existence of key success factors that one would consider in implementing a successful business mentoring program. Among the commonalities can be cited:

- Availability of a pool of mentors;
- Mentor has substantial experience relevant to the mentee;
- Effective screening of mentor and mentee;

- Orientation of mentor and mentee regarding the program;
- Mentee is responsible to draw developmental plan and objectives;
- Accountability of the mentee regarding the outcomes;
- Agreement between the mentor and mentee regarding plans and goals;
- Close intervention of program coordinator in initiating rapport and monitoring relationship between mentor and mentee;
- Periodic reporting to the coordinator of the evolution of the relationship and the progress regarding developmental goals;
- Agreement on frequency and regularity of mentoring meetings;
- Establishment of proper timing regarding the duration of the mentoring relationship.

It is perfectly normal that a program bears its own specificities in regard to the assumptions held in the design phase. In this context, the following differences can be found in the design and implementation:

- Duration of the mentoring program and the frequency and length of the meetings;
- Gender of mentor and mentee;
- Fee paid by the mentee, status and recruitment mode of the mentor;
- Expectation that the mentee plays the role of mentor at a later stage;
- Agreement on confidentiality;
- Learning objectives and contents.

In addition to the above key success factors that a strategic mentoring program might require to pursue its objectives, it is important to envisage as well other elements that can potentially undermined the effectiveness of a mentoring program. Among those elements are:

- A failure to develop a sense purpose and direction expressed in terms of end-results for the program;
- A failure to strategically choose the participants, namely mentees, mentors and coordinator;
- A failure to define leading indicators and establish a feedback system for continual improvement;
- A failure to put in place pre and post assessment to monitor progress.

Therefore, the design, planning and implementation needs to be carefully thought through in order to avoid those pitfalls.

CHAPTER III

DESIGNING AN EFFECTIVE STRATEGIC

MENTORING PROGRAM

This chapter addresses different elements that are important when setting up a strategic mentoring program. Firstly, it considers the foundation of a program through the establishment of the vision, the mission and the goals. Secondly, it outlines the content of an effective plan and organizational structure for a strategic mentoring program. Thirdly, it addresses how such a program is to be assessed and structured as to promote double-loop learning.

a. The foundation of an effective mentoring program

It is said that building an organization or a program operates from the philosophy upon which a house is built, namely by planning or visioning and laying down the foundation. Setting up a program requires visioning as to determine the end-results before starting to implement or perform activities. In fact, building a house can be considered effective only if it has been subjected to proper planning. Planning helps discern the important questions that a mentoring program may face which can help address the future of the mentoring program. Those questions are the following:

- Why should this program exist? What are the needs which would not be met if it did not exist?
- What is the program's specialty? What makes it unique?
- What are the resources the program has at its disposal? What are the possible limitations in regards to the available resources?
- Why should small business leaders join this mentoring program?
- What are the values or behaviors that are required for success? What are the qualities that mentors and mentees should possess?
- In which direction shall the program go? What type of mentoring programs and formats shall it adopt?
- What is it seeking to accomplish? What behavioral changes does this program aim at promoting?

Above everything else, it is important that the mentoring program is built on a solid foundation to ensure its effectiveness as well as its sustainability; and part of the process of building a solid foundation is the fact of defining a mission and a vision for the program (see appendix).

1. Mission Statement

As the genesis of all planning processes, a mission statement represents the strategic direction of a program and is used as a guide for activities to be implemented. The mission does not refer to a particular objective, but rather defines the reason for being or the essential purpose of the mentoring program. It provides meaning to all the activities that will be undertaken. Allison and Kaye put it in perspective by saying:" *failure to state and communicate an organization's purpose (in "ends" terminology) can lead an organization to inadvertently restrict its effectiveness.*" In other words, the mission statement constitutes a key element in the success of a given program. More specifically, it provides guidance to the stakeholders, board, mentors, mentees, staff, etc., in answering questions such as: why should this program exist? Whom is it serving? Where is it implemented? What is it trying to accomplish? And what are the values that the program must hold onto in implementing its activities?

- **Why should the program exist?** A person, an organization or a program must come to an understanding of his/her or its identity. A program must strategically define itself, thus creating meaning for what it intends to do. Meaning is the necessary ingredient that motivates people or organizations to move forward. It is essential that any program and especially a strategic mentoring program address the above question before stepping into mentoring activities. The answer to this question can serve as a powerful motivation for the existing and potential stakeholders involved in such a program, allowing them to be aware that they are involved in something bigger than themselves. It provides meaning to activities implemented.

  In the case of a small business development program, it could be to assess the constraints that hinder small business leaders' effectiveness or prevent them from taking advantages of opportunities in their environment. Had those issues or opportunities been dealt with, the small businesses would create the job and wealth expected of them. Therefore, the mission statement of a strategic mentoring program in Haiti could express how the economic condition of the country would improve because of its intervention. And that could be a convincing argument outlined during events to recruit volunteer mentors and personnel.

- **Who does the program wants to serve?** No program can be effective by being all things to everybody, nor can a program be effective when it is solely serving its owners. At this stage, the program needs to have a focus on whom it is strategically serving. In a society characterized by activities and motion without purpose, it is easy to forget who we are ultimately serving. Thus, a program needs to develop a profile of all its stakeholders, especially the beneficiaries. A mentoring program can not be designed as a one-size-fits-all. Not everyone has the same needs and the organization or program has limited resources. Thus, identifying or defining the participants at all levels is one important step. A profile of participants can answer questions such as:

  o Who are they? What is their average age? What is their gender?
  o Where are they located?
  o What are their needs, talents and resources?
  o What is their current situation?
  o Why is the program important for them?
  o What are their expectations regarding a mentoring program?
  o How can they contribute to the success of the program?

- **Where will the program be implemented?** The specificities of the place (city, country, region, etc.) where the program is implemented are of great importance. A mentoring model that worked perfectly in Belgium might not work in Haiti as the prevailing conditions are not the same. Therefore, a model cannot be copied in one environment and pasted in another. It needs to undergo certain adaptation to make sure that it is culturally relevant to the people it aims at serving. For example, while for certain cultures it is normal that a female plays the role of mentor to a mentee who is of male gender, this is not the case in some other cultures. If it is allowed somewhere that the mentor be younger than the mentee, it is not acceptable everywhere. Race can be a sensitive issue, as well. In Haiti, a white person is sometimes associated with wealth and his/her presence in a program as a mentor is likely to convey a message that money will be part of the exchange and thus undermine the mentoring relationship, if it is not addressed upfront. That is why an intelligent mentoring program carefully considers the context where it is implemented.

- **What is the program trying to accomplish?** The program must be clear about the goals that are being pursued. Chrisman and Leslie investigated various types of problems encountered by small business leaders and classified them as administrative issues (dealing with the organization of a business and its ability to acquire and develop resources), operating issues (dealing with the functional areas of a business, such as marketing, production, and operations) and strategic issues (dealing with the overall objectives and goals of an organization). It could be important for the program to decide upfront, in its area of intervention, what will be addressed and what will not be as far as business issues are concerned. This step is crucial in the outline of the profile of the mentors and the subject matters or curriculum which will be used in the context of the mentoring relationship.

It is crucial that a mentoring program defines its level of involvement in assisting small business leaders to address those issues in their businesses. Should it focus solely on administrative issues, operating issues or strategic ones? Or should it address all of them? The main question is about the focus of the program, namely management competency development or leadership development, for they are the most common issues faced by small business leaders. This aspect is very important for a mentoring program for it determines the type of structure, the format, the content and outline of the mentoring sessions, the outputs and outcomes, as well as the indicators that will be used to monitor progress and evaluate its effectiveness.

- **What should be the core values of the program?** In pursuing its goals, the mentoring program should be careful at defining at the outset the values that will guide its decisions vis-à-vis the mentors, mentees, staff and other stakeholders. More importantly, the program needs to determine how it will assess the relationships between the mentors and mentees. In other words, defining the values that the mentors and mentees will have to adhere to if they are to participate in the mentoring program. Those expressed values can be useful during stages such as identification, selection, recruitment, and termination because they talk about how the mission will be carried out and the nature of the means that will be utilized in so doing. Most literature on mentoring highlights values such as mutual respect, confidentiality, empathy, discipline, openness of mind, flexibility, etc. It is important that every single component of a mentoring program be defined. This assures that the program takes the stated values into account.

The above elements are to be represented in what is called the mission statement of the mentoring program. It is important that all stakeholders be aware of this mission as it encapsulates the reason for the existence of the program—the what, why, and how. The mission not only constitutes a powerful motivation for the program itself as it provides meaning, direction and focus to the activities undertaken, but also serves as a signpost that addresses the questions that potential participants may ask themselves before joining. Arguing about mission, Jack Welch stated that: "*it requires companies to make choices about people, investment, and other resources, and it prevents them from falling into the common trap of asserting they will be all things to all people at all times.*" Stakeholders might be asking themselves other important questions such as where is this program going or what is the desired situation or impact the program is striving to accomplish? In other words, what is the vision behind this program?

It is not recommended to start implementing a strategic mentoring program prior to answering these questions. But the answers are not just to be printed on a sheet of paper and hung on a wall. They need to be put into practice so that the program is congruent with what it claims to do. The mission statement also needs to be consulted when major decisions are to be made or when changes are monitored in the environment where the program is taking place. This process ensures that the mission stays relevant to what the program intends to do.

2. Shared vision

Along with the mission that defines the essential purpose of the program, it is important as well to cast a vision which defines the direction where the program is heading. A compelling vision attracts the necessary resources for its implementation. Walt Disney said, "If you can dream it, you can do it." An effective program starts indeed with a vision. It is not good to start moving without a sense of direction or purpose. Max De Pre stated that: "*the first responsibility of a leader is to define reality.*" In support to that statement, Warren Bennis emphasized that: "*All leaders have the capacity to create a compelling vision, one that takes people to a new place, and then to translate that vision into reality.*"

Ironically, how can a program that aims at leadership competency development not have a vision for itself while the first expected quality of a leader is the aptitude to define and communicate a vision? How would such a program manage to recruit or motivate participants? How would the stakeholders support such a program without knowing where it is going ultimately? How worthy is it to follow a program that is directed to nowhere but activities? Answers to those questions can obviously be found in the definition and communication of a vision for the mentoring program.

Defining a vision can be described as actualizing the impact or the changes a program is seeking to accomplish in the future as a result of the activities to be implemented. What expectation does the program have for the profile of the participants when they graduate from the mentoring program after three years? What will success look like? Because they have been participating in the mentoring program, what will they have accomplished in their personal and organizational life? How will the economic landscape be different as a result of the implementation of the mentoring program? Finally, how will the world become a better place because of their involvement in this type of program?

Those are the questions that can be useful in the elaboration of a vision for an effective mentoring program. And they should be answered in ways that allow others to envision the future. As Jim Collins puts it: "*The envisioned future must, on the one hand, convey a sense of concreteness—something vivid and real; you can see it, touch it, and feel it. On the other hand, it portrays a time yet unrealized—a dream, hope or aspiration.*" Warren Bennis, cited by Jean-Pierre Bal asserts that: "*a vision should speak to the needs of others in the organization, to the strivings and hopes that may be unexpressed but held within. If it touches their longings, if it resonates with what is deeply felt, it will have the power of a vision.*" This translates that the power in a vision can be unleashed when the latter is effectively communicated.

Like the mission, a well articulated vision has the capacity to motivate people. It is imperative that a vision for a program be communicated. And this is not a one-way communication, but rather a constructive dialogue where key stakeholders get the opportunity to refine, share their inputs, shape, see their role in the vision and ultimately make it their own. John Kotter put it in perspective when he said: "*If you can not communicate the vision to someone in five minutes or less and get a reaction that signifies both understanding and interest, you are not yet done with this phase of the transformation process.*"

It will be easier for an organization to attract mentors, sponsors and mentees when it is able to display or communicate a clear and compelling vision for its mentoring program. Once shared, the vision operates as a covenant that binds key stakeholders in accomplishing the vision. More importantly, the vision must allow one to envision the feasibility of its implementation. Deriving specific goals from the vision is one means by which energy can be mobilized, thus making sense of the activities that people will be taking part in.

Referring to the extraordinary leadership of the Antarctic explorer Ernest Shackleton, Dennis N.T. Perkins, argued that effective leadership channels its energy in pursuing a vision as well as medium and short term goals. Indeed, it allows key stakeholders to celebrate short term victories and enhance their motivation as they are moving towards a bigger goal—the vision. Audet and Couteret assess that setting short term goals simplify the measurement and the monitoring of progress and more importantly, it provides the opportunity to review and rectify the strategy undertaken. In the case of a mentoring program, goals could be both organizational and programmatic. Programmatic goals will be, of course, articulated in accordance with the learning modules and processes that will constitute the competency or skills development as determined in the program's mission. Whereas, the organizational goals address how the program should be structured to facilitate the accomplishment of its programmatic goals.

When the vision has been broken down into sizable goals outlined in terms of outputs and outcomes, it is possible to track what the program has accomplished through the various activities implemented and the budget that has facilitated the implementation of the activities. This aspect of the program is very important to the program participants themselves as well as to the other key stakeholders like the funding agencies.

Furthermore, the successful management of a mentoring program, the monitoring of progress, the satisfaction of the mentors and mentees, and the accountability of the leadership depend largely on the establishment of goals. And, as often said, they have to be specific, measurable and action-oriented, realistic and timely. In defining goals, the program's leadership should envision at the same time the results as well as the indicators that help monitor progress. This aspect will be thoroughly addressed in the third part. Finally, the mission and vision, considered as the corner stone of an effective mentoring program, can be used within the framework of a conversation guide for activities to promote and market the program. And more importantly, the defined mission and vision will determine, to a great extent, the number and profile of the mentors and mentees, as well as the type and format that the mentoring program should espouse in regards to its effectiveness.

As the mission, vision and goals are defined, the program must decide on the appropriate structure which would allow them to be fully integrated and implemented in the best way possible. Therefore, a strategy needs to be formulated to activate the program. This is exactly where the commonalities found in the mentoring programs come into play; for those commonalities can be seen as a pattern or a pathway which leads to the implementation of a successful mentoring program. That is the reason why they are called key success factors.

b. Strategies, organization and structure

The foundation of a mentoring program has been laid. It is time now to address the necessary structure that would support the implementation of the program strategies and activities. The key to the design of strategies to accomplish the vision lies in an effective targeting of mentors, mentees and a program coordinator, as well as the definition of process and structure which will guide and facilitate genuine relationships with the parties involved. Those elements along with the statements of mission and vision need to be carefully planned to ensure that a strategic mentoring program bring about the expected results or changes in the personal and professional lives of small business leaders. The role that small business leaders can play in the economy is dependent upon the intelligence in the design and implementation of facilitated assistance programs, such as strategic mentoring.

1. Effective targeting

If an effective mentoring program cannot be all things, to everybody at all times, the one thing it needs to do is to define a screening process to select and recruit the key participants, namely the mentors, the mentees and the program coordinator. The success of a mentoring program relies on the accuracy with which the participants are chosen. And the screening process varies based on the nature of the participants in the program. That is why it is important to consider each participant separately.

On the mentors

A mentoring program will make sure to have at its disposal a pool of mentors. Any small business leader who joins a mentoring program expects to benefit from the availability and support of a mentor. And that wish should be granted. That is why, at the outset, it is important to check the number of mentors available in the program's database before signing up mentees. Since the number of mentors will greatly influence the management of the program, it has to be planned as well. If that database does not exist, it needs to be created. In so doing, creating a mentoring program for small businesses would require that each mentor have sufficient business experience. A repertoire of potential mentors can be drawn from members of business associations, chambers of commerce, business school alumni or other organized groups. Targeting groups helps reduce the public relations budget in comparison to marketing conducted on a face to face basis. It is more cost-efficient to address people within an association instead of individually.

Starting from these types of institutions is important for many reasons. Firstly, some of those institutions sometimes influence their members to invest in philanthropy. Since the mentor will be a volunteer, it is a plus if he/she is already sensitive to concepts such as social responsibilities or corporate citizenship as a way to give back to society. Secondly, word-of-mouth is one effective tool to get a message across. Mentors are good at recruiting other mentors in their immediate network; so being in an association provides that proximity.

However, Handord acknowledged, in regards to recruiting mentors, that people are more likely to volunteer when they feel they are being asked to get involved personally and when they are asked repeatedly. That is why face-to-face invitations are a critical strategy in recruiting mentors. Finally, senior students with business experience can be equally good candidates to serve as mentors to small business leaders if the latter are not sensitive to age matters. A research conducted by Finkelstein, Allen and Rhoton revealed that reverse-age mentorship could create situations of discomfort for an older individual being guided by a junior organizational member.

If the matter related to the quantity of mentors is important, that of the quality is even more important. Grove and Huon posit that the success of a mentoring program depends greatly on the skills of the mentor. In the same vein, the National Mentoring Partners added that, beside numbers, a mentoring program needs to focus on how well the prospective mentor can relate to the mentee and fit in with the program goals.

Therefore, it is crucial that a set of selection criteria be used in the process to determine who is more likely to be an effective mentor that reflects the mission and vision of the program.

Profiling mentors is a must. Most literature about mentors concedes that a mentor will have developed aptitudes and qualifications such as active listening, sense of commitment, empathy, leadership, integrity, humility, etc.

More specifically, Edgcomb and Malm developed a list of qualifications that are needed for a mentor:

- a desire to help;
- positive, past experience being mentored formally;
- or informally; experience as a business person with a track record of helping others develop their skills;
- time and energy to devote to the relationship;
- current business and/or technological knowledge and skills;
- willingness to learn; and
- demonstrated coaching, counseling, facilitating and networking skills.

As the targeting is taking place, the mentoring program will make sure to develop a conversation guide to use in meeting with the potential mentors. The conversation guide needs to outline not only the mission and vision of the program, but also it needs to emphasize the value or benefits for the mentor if they make a decision to enroll, especially when the program is non-compensatory. Last, but not least, is the (social) recognition system that should be put in place to encourage and retain mentors in the program. Once the program has at its disposal a database of potential mentors, it needs to consider selecting the appropriate mentees to initiate the mentoring relationships.

On the mentees

If the success of a mentoring program depends on the efficacy of the mentors, it depends greatly on the readiness of the mentees to participate in such programs. The mentee, like the mentor, needs to have a profile that is suitable for mentoring. It is believed that not all small business leaders are ready for a formal mentoring program. In fact, a facilitated mentoring program would require certain qualifications that unfortunately are not available in the skills' repertoire of some business owners. Among those qualifications can be cited, self-directedness and entrepreneurial agility.

It can happen that craftsmanship is mistaken for entrepreneurship. While the former defines the capacity of a business owner to fabricate a product, the latter encapsulates a range of skills such as risk-taking, decision-making, visioning, innovating, etc. A mentee will succeed in a facilitated mentoring program when he/she is able to develop a developmental agenda or goals and take full responsibility for the outcomes. A certain internal locus of control is important in the mentoring process. And it starts with the question about where do I want to go/be and how do I get there. In other words, the mentoring program needs to have the mentee be accountable for progress.

That is why the same rigor that is used in selecting the mentor should also be applied to the person of the mentee. To begin with, a mentoring program has to be established around small business leaders' needs. Therefore, it is the responsibility of a program to assess the current and future needs of its prospective mentees in order to serve them more effectively. Chrisman and Leslie's classification of issues faced by small business leaders (administrative, operating and strategic) can be a starting point, but the assessment needs to go further than that. If it is true that not all business leaders are able to accurately identify and express their needs, it is up to the program to help them with this assessment.

However, the needs assessment that is conducted with and on behalf of a group of small business leaders is not a guarantee that they should automatically be qualified to participate in the program. Like the mentor, the mentee has to undergo a selection process. Murray stated that: "*the primary criterion for selection is that the protégé be motivated to develop different and greater competencies. No matter how formally or informally the relationship is structured, if the protégé is not motivated, nothing will be gained.*" In other words, the mentee needs to be self-directed and open to change.

While most literature on mentoring talks about what makes an effective mentor, very few talk about characteristics of the mentee. Nevertheless, some characteristics are expressed in the literature such as: receptiveness to feedback, commitment to the mentoring relationship, time available, entrepreneurial agility, ability to identify goals, etc. In contrast to the mentor, Edgcomb and Malm retain the following abilities that a mentee should have to be considered ready for mentoring:

- clear and realistic expectations of what a mentoring relationship can provide;
- defined set of business issues or challenges for which advice is needed;
- willingness and ability to provide time and energy to the relationship, and to pursuing the recommendations made by the mentor;
- self-confidence;

- demonstrated capacity to set goals and implement plans to achieve them; and
- willingness to be accountable to the mentor.

Another important aspect concerning the mentee is how knowledgeable they are and how they learn best. It is then the responsibility of the mentor via the program to develop a tailored curriculum that fits the mentee. And this is where the program needs to benefit from the intervention of a key staff person to help facilitate the mentor/mentee relationship and make sure that both the mentor and mentee get the most out of this relationship. In that case, the role of a program coordinator is not to be neglected and must be properly selected as well.

Dr. Jean Rhodes, cited by the National Mentoring Partners, stated that: "*the most significant predicator of positive mentoring results in whether mentors and mentees share a close, trusting relationship. Such relationships do not just happen. They need ongoing support and monitoring, particularly during early stages, to ensure that the relationships do not terminate prematurely.*" This is when the program coordinator steps in as a significant third party. The coordinator is the glue that holds the program together; much rests on his/her shoulders as the backbone of the program. While the success of a mentoring program is largely dependent upon both the mentor and the mentee, the intervention of a coordinator cannot be underestimated.

On the program coordinator

The same scrutiny that is necessary when selecting mentors and mentees needs to be applied to the person of the program coordinator. The program coordinator plays an important role in the process and can be considered the backbone for the mentoring program. The program coordinator is the one that ensures that mentors and mentees are on track in regards to developmental goals and the agreed upon action plan. This position is even more crucial when the mentor, supposedly a business person, lacks time beyond the mentoring relationship to get involved in the administrative matters necessary for follow-up.

It is expected that the program coordinator be skilled in non-profit as well as for-profit management and leadership. The program coordinator will need to relate to funding agencies or donors, business associations, business schools, small business leaders and other stakeholders. This position cannot be underestimated for it plays an integral part in the early process of selecting and recruiting mentors and mentees and it is very important to the establishment of a winning structure for the strategic business mentoring program.

Referring to practitioners with experience in facilitating mentoring program, Edgcomb and Malm have identified the following important design considerations which fall naturally under the responsibility of the program coordinator:

- identifying characteristics that may qualify a small business leader for a mentoring program;
- developing a mechanism to select and recruit appropriate mentors and mentees;
- clarifying expectations of both mentors and mentees regarding their roles and responsibilities;
- designing a process for matching mentors and mentees;
- structuring a process with a clear beginning, middle and end, and with a mechanism for early exit based on the assessment of the participants; and
- establishing ongoing program monitoring and support to the program participants.

In fact, the program coordinator's role is to render operational the mission and vision of the mentoring program. Therefore, management and leadership skills are a must for this position. Usually, the position requires the capacity to get involved both in the non-profit and for-profit setting. On the one hand, the program coordinator needs to facilitate the design of program plan which underlines specific goals framed as outputs and outcomes of the program, strategies and means to achieve the goals, indicators to monitor progress and a mechanism for ongoing supervision and support, follow-up and record keeping. Those skills are very relevant to the management of a not-for-profit program.

In addition, the program coordinator needs to be quite knowledgeable in business matters. It would be an asset if he does have a repertoire of business contacts as the program targets small business leaders as mentees and mostly mentors with extended business experience. In addition to that, Murray suggests looking for the following skills and qualifications in a potential program coordinator:

- good practical analysis;
- public-relations;
- planning, organization and leadership;
- negotiation and judgment;
- administration, structuring and facilitation.

The need for those skills and qualifications confirms the importance of an effective targeting of the program coordinator, like in the case of the mentors and the mentees. More importantly, the program will make sure to consider that the key players share the mission, values and vision of the program. Jim Collins, observed that: "*In determining "the right people", the good-to-great companies placed greater weight on character attributes than on specific educational background, practical skills, specialized knowledge and work experience. Not that specific knowledge and skills are unimportant but they viewed that these traits are more teachable (or at least learnable), whereas they believed dimensions like character, work ethic, basic intelligence, dedication to fulfilling commitments, and values are more ingrained."* Both skills and character attributes will be crucial in the development and implementation of the necessary process and structure to ensure the effectiveness of the mentoring program. Therefore, they need to be taken into consideration in the program coordinator's hiring process.

2. Process and structure

Structuring the mentoring program is important as it determines the efficacy and satisfaction resulted from mentors-mentees relationships. In fact, bringing together a mentor and a mentee does not often result in a positive outcome for both parties. The literature on mentoring also considers the dark side or negative aspects of facilitated mentoring programs. Kram et al. cited by O'Neil and Sankowsky speculated about various negative aspects such as unmet expectations, possible loss of self-esteem, frustration, blocked opportunity, and a sense of betrayal for the mentee. The mentor as well can be frustrated when the performance of the mentee is unable to meet the mentor's expectations or a personality conflict exists.

According to Elby et al. cited by O'Neil and Sankowsky all those setbacks that can contribute to creating dysfunction in the mentoring relationship are found mostly in formal mentoring programs rather than informal programs. However, they are found mostly in internal mentoring programs, rather than in external mentoring programs. Nevertheless, they also need to be taken into consideration in the design of the mentoring program. Therefore, the structure and process must be carefully planned and implemented so that all the parties involved benefit from the positive aspects of a mentoring program while mitigating the risk of emergence of the negative ones.

Building a structure and defining a process for a mentoring relationship needs to be intelligently designed in order to ensure the viability of the program. This structuring must make provision for training and orientation sessions to mentors and mentees, facilitating the transition process from one stage to another in the mentoring relationship phase and ensuring proper documentation of the process, outputs and outcomes of the mentoring relationships.

Orientation sessions

Although in the mentors selection criteria it is recommended to seek those who have benefited from positive, past experiences being mentored formally or informally, it is not always easy to find prospective mentors who meet that criteria. It would also be good to find mentees who have benefited from that same experience in other areas of their lives, but this is more a matter of wishful thinking. O'Neil and Sankowsky assert that, from a practical standpoint, mentoring is not something that all leaders are necessarily trained to do well. In addition to that, Audet and Couteret believe that it is the program coordinator's responsibility to not only set the ground rules and guidelines, but also prepare the pathway for the mentoring relationship.

At the outset, the prospective participants in a mentoring relationship need to be aware of what it entails. And for this, training and orientation sessions are needed. Some programs would conduct the session with mentors and mentees at the same time. But it is more effective that each participant get a sense of what the mentoring program is about before engaging in a matching process. Matching can sometimes be based on the needs expressed by the mentee and the suitability of the mentors to accompany the mentee or just on commonalities or areas of interest between the parties.

Since it is not obvious, most of the time, if mentors and mentees have been involved in a mentoring relationship before they start the program, the training and orientation sessions help them address and deal with the context and challenges in relation to a mentoring relationship. Such training needs to take place in the early stage before entering into the mentoring relationship. Some participants in this training and orientation should be given the option to withdraw from the program if they assess that they cannot operate with the values set forth by the program. Therefore, those who decide to join the program are motivated and fully committed to it since they are aware of what it entails or what it requires from them.

Grove and Huon et al. suggest that training sessions need to cover the following topics:

- the rationale and objective of the mentoring program;
- the role of the mentor; accountability and responsibility of the mentor and the mentee;
- the role of the program coordinator and the program's policies and procedures;
- how to facilitate a mentoring session and develop learning contents;

- the design and format of learning or moral contracts based on developmental needs and the action plan;
- confidentiality and liability parameters;
- barriers to communication, building rapport and empathy;
- principles of adult learning and education;
- ways to assess and improve the mentoring process;
- the level of commitment expected;
- the duration of the mentoring program, the frequency and location of the meetings;
- process for handling unexpected or planned termination of the mentoring relationship.

It is important to also address cross-cultural and racial issues during the training sessions when the mentoring program participants differ in those areas. In addition to that, Cloke and Goldsmith recommend that mentors be trained to develop their skills in listening, feedback, strategic planning, conflict resolution, and changing organizational culture. These different topics can be outlined in a written format so that mentor and mentee have access to it at will or refer to it during the relationship when need be. It is crucial that all the parties understand and learn from the topics covered during the training session before they engage in the mentoring relationship at the implementation phase.

On the mentoring stages

The training or orientation session is what prepares the mentors and mentees to be ready to implement the mentoring relationship with the support of the program coordinator. In regards to the mentoring relationship process, Handford stated that mentoring follows a lifecycle which involves five phases, namely initiation, cultivation, maturation, separation and redefinition.

Cloke and Goldsmith posit that a strategic mentoring process starts with mentors and mentees collaboratively defining their relationship, developing a clear understanding of the differences in their personalities and communication styles, sharing criteria for success and defining boundaries and possibilities of working together. In other terms, during **the initiation phase**, the focus of the parties is that of establishing working terms. In so doing, the mentee communicates with the mentor the developmental needs for which the mentoring is sought while seeking inputs from the latter.

The development plan, according to Murray, can espouse the format commonly used for performance planning, objective setting and action planning. It can also establish the duration of the mentoring relationship. As the plan will include outcomes, time lines, required resources and progress checkpoints, the involvement of the program coordinator is crucial. It is recommended that the mentoring program creates a development plan format or a set of guidelines to harmonize all the interventions. This action plan serves as an agreement between all parties regarding the description of skills to be learned and practiced, the type of activities that will provide this practice and the time and frequency of meetings and feedback sessions. Such a document which conveys common understanding and expresses expectations regarding the involvement of each party is very important for the success of the relationship.

Based on the expectations set forth, the parties can now engage in the **cultivation of the relationship** which is the second phase. At this stage, both mentor and mentee are actively collaborating in accomplishing the goals in a learning environment where respect, support and trust prevail. But as Hersey and Blanchard put it: "*The goals should be set high* *enough so that a person has to stretch to reach them but low enough so that they can be attainable.*" That's why the goal setting process needs to be joint effort between mentors and mentees. Via the agreed upon mentoring format, the mentor provides advice, guidance and developmental feedback to the mentee while the latter is receptively active in the process. All the participants, namely mentor, mentee and program coordinator will make sure to evaluate the process regularly and make corrections when need be.

As the mentee develops the necessary skills and competencies outlined in the developmental plan, the mentor may step back and challenge the mentee to take more responsibilities. This is **the maturation phase,** described by the mentee's ability to move towards independence as a result of the capacities developed. This identification of developed capacities is first the responsibility of the mentee because self-confidence is important in the process, and even more so, when the mentee is responsible for his/her own personal growth and development. It is the responsibility of the mentee to identify the capacities he is growing in. In this way the mentee builds self-confidence and takes ownership of his/her own personal growth and development.

The separation phase indicates that the mentee is able to fly by him/herself. It is a time of celebration. The mentee has developed a sense of security in regards to the abilities developed which have been seen at work both at a personal and organizational level. Cloke and Goldsmith said that: "*The object of strategic mentoring is thus for the mentors to become increasingly invisible and irrelevant to the mentees . . . allowing the latter to make their own decisions, experience their own mistakes, and discover their own path through the maze.*" At that phase, most of the developmental needs have been met. The mentor, the program coordinator and the mentee agree on the performance and progress made by the latter in regards to the agreed upon developmental needs and action plan knowing that all of them were involved in documenting the process. At this stage, it is proper for the parties to bring the mentoring sessions to an end.

Concluding the mentoring session does not always mean the termination of the personal relationship that the mentee has developed over time with both the mentor and the program coordinator. Rather, this starts the phase called redefinition where the mentee or small business leader is invited to step into the program as a mentor and develop an equal relationship with the other parties. It is obvious that because the mentee is now a mentor in the program, he/she is likely to be considered an asset in the effectiveness of the mentoring program; and more so, when that mentor is willing to share his/her story with others in promotional events to recruit other mentors. In this particular context, graduation means moving from a mentee to a mentor position.

A mentoring relationship is not static. It evolves with the participants in the process. It is important to define a mechanism to monitor where the participants are in the process and what is to be done at every level. Every step needs to be planned and acknowledged by all the parties involved, namely the mentor, the mentee and the program coordinator. While the mentoring relationship needs a timeframe or duration to prevent dependency from taking place in the process, it is not necessary to specify the time it takes to move from one phase to another in the process.

The participants should be given the freedom to progress at their own speed and pace. This process is very important especially when mentoring is understood as experiential learning and operates within the parameters of adult learning and education. Besides, it is the role of the mentor to assess what needs to be communicated to the mentee. And the rule of thumb is, not too much too soon. It may be difficult to determine at the outset how long a mentee will take to move from one phase to another. However, it is important to put in place a monitoring system to assess the movement of the mentees through the different phases of the program.

On the feedback system

The success or sustainability of a volunteer-based program lies in the capacity of its promoters to actively market it and attract key stakeholders. The best way to market a program is to collect success stories from the participants. It is important for the program to design a mechanism to collect feedback from the participants on a regular basis. The feedback can be useful to provide details where needed as to elaborate narratives to publish outside via the program's newsletters and promotional materials such as brochures and flyers or other mediums like Internet or television, etc. The National Mentoring Partners recommends a form of promotion that is practical and appropriate for each audience by separating successful mentor-related information from mentee-related information. However, only the circumstances can tell which one is important to display or if a combination of both would produce the winning strategy.

In order to do that, the program coordinator needs to be present at all stages in the process to gather accurate information both from the mentors and mentees. The collected information can be used as well for the accountability of the program vis-à-vis the donors or other key stakeholders.

A thorough documentation system needs to be designed to support the public relations activities or communication efforts. Too many times the success a program is experiencing stays with the insiders or the sole participants. A program cannot endure and impact society at large without the involvement of community members who are qualified to participate. Besides, as the program shares its success with a larger constituency, it is likely to receive feedback or best practices from others that may even boost its effectiveness. It is therefore important for the mentoring program to identify partners who are involved in a different capacity (academia, chambers of commerce, consulting firms, etc.), but in relation to the developmental needs or the success of small business leaders.

Since the program will need to be perfected over time, it is necessary to put in place a feedback system in order to monitor every step of the process so that corrective actions can be undertaken. Once again, the parties involved need to carefully document the relationship and make that information available to the program coordinator on a regular basis. Some of that information can be articulated into narratives, in the case of success stories, and be disseminated both in the program to encourage the participants and outside of the program to motivate potential mentors and mentees as well as donor partners. The marketing of such programs is more effective when it is based around success stories and best practices because they help capture in real words what the program is about and what it can do in the personal and organizational lives of the participants. In fact, the program's evaluation needs to focus on both the process and the impact in order to improve the quality of the intervention, as well as to assess its contribution in society or the economy in general.

The mentoring program needs to come up with tools to gauge the condition of the mentee or mentor/mentee relationship and the overall effectiveness of the program. One way to accomplish this is to develop parameters for evaluation of performance and impact.

c. Evaluation of performance and impact

It is said: "*if you can not measure it properly, you will not be able to manage properly.*" The manner in which the mentoring program will be evaluated is as important as the definition of mission and vision statements, goals and strategies. Evaluation serves multiple purposes; on the one hand, it helps portray how well the program fulfilled its mission and vision and what changes have occurred in the personal and professional lives of those participating in the program.

On the other hand, it facilitates the reinforcement of positive behaviors, while assessing those that are not, seeking possible ways to undertake corrective actions and foster a learning culture in the program. In addition, the evaluation allows the program to be accountable to the key stakeholders involved in supporting its implementation. Basically, the evaluation addresses how well the program is being run at its different stages or life-cycles and ultimately addresses its overall effectiveness. In this context, the evaluation needs to consider both the process and the outcomes of the mentoring program with a focus on learning what would promote continual refinement and more effectiveness.

1. Process evaluation

While the mentors and the mentees are expected to monitor the evolution of the relationship by themselves, this does not exclude the fact that the program coordinator will need to conduct an evaluation about the health and effectiveness of the mentoring process. Some mentoring programs only have their participants filling an exit interview questionnaire at the end. However, Handford argued that the ongoing process monitoring is one of the factors that contribute to the success of a mentoring relationship.

The monitoring of the implementation process is important for the effectiveness of all the parties involved in the program, namely the mentor, the mentee and the program coordinator, even when the monitoring rests on the shoulders of the latter. The process evaluation, also called formative evaluation, allows the participants to develop a better appreciation of the expected goals by making judgments about whether they are realistic or not. This monitoring can happen formally or informally, individually or collectively. Whatever the form espoused, it is not be associated with controlling. It would not help the program to be perceived as such.

The monitoring is more effective if conducted in a participatory manner, and it can take place via different questionnaires that are administered to the program participants or via focus groups where all involved are called to reflect on the mentoring relationships. The most important thing is to assist the mentor and mentee to cultivate the habit of reflecting on the relationship and sharing their feedback to the program via the coordinator. In fact, the program coordinator needs to design both a reporting and feedback system and a mechanism to integrate the findings back to the program to ensure that it works to accomplish its mission and vision.

Indeed, it is the responsibility of the program coordinator to routinely or periodically meet with the mentor and the mentee to gather their feedback regarding the development of the mentoring relationship. Murray recommends that the program develops forms, that record experiences and actions that should be completed by both the mentor and the mentee at agreed intervals during the process. These forms would typically focus on how the mentoring program worked. Besides the use of forms, the assessment can be conducted in a focus group format to allow more interactions with the participants. In fact, focus groups can be used as a check-up system to monitor the satisfaction of the parties in regard to the mentoring relationship. In the check-up or review sessions, the program will ensure that the satisfaction of the mentors and mentees are properly assessed in regards to the mentoring process on a regular basis. That is why the intervention of the program coordinator is critical to the success of the mentoring process. Typical questions to ask in such sessions could be expressed as follows:

Mentor and Mentee's Questionnaires

Mentor's questions	Mentee's questions
- How satisfied are you with the mentoring relationship so far? Why do you feel like that? - Are your expectations met to some extent? Why? - What are the things that you are most satisfied about? What are the things that you are not happy with? - What have you learned personally in the mentoring relationship? - How do you compare the success of the mentoring relationship in regards to the mentee's developmental needs and action plan? - How do you monitor the progress of the mentee in regards to agreed upon goals? - How often do you meet with the mentee? How is the mentee showing responsibility for his/her own growth? - What possible changes which were not planned have you witnessed in the mentee? What are the possible causes? - Are you envisioning a possible time period where the mentee can graduate from the mentoring program? Why? What are the indicators that motivate your answer? - What are the factors that you consider helpful in the success of the mentoring relationship? - What are the factors that you think hinder the success of the relationship? - How do you think those negative factors should be addressed? - Do you envision revisiting and revising the action plan with the mentee? - How can the coordinator assist you to improve the mentoring relationship?	- How satisfied are you regarding the mentoring relationship? Why? - Are your expectations met? Why? - What are the things that you are most satisfied with in your mentoring relationship? What are the things that you are not happy with? - How do you compare yourself in regards to your entry into the program? - Where are you now in regards to your developmental needs and action plan? - What are the unexpected changes you have monitored? - What are the factors you think have been positive in the changes (expected and unexpected) you've monitored? - How often do you meet with your mentor? - What are the factors you consider as roadblocks to a more effective mentoring relationship? - How can those obstacles be addressed? Do you have a plan for that? - How can the mentor assist you in mitigating the negative factors that influence the mentoring relationship? Have you addressed that with your mentor? - How can the coordinator assist you? - Where do you see yourself as far as graduation is concerned?

In addition, it could be an opportunity for the mentor and mentee to revise the goals that have been set and maybe develop new goals that were not defined in the initial action plan. It makes sense to do so as the mentoring relationship has to evolve since it is being implemented in a dynamic environment. Not only can the goals be revised at this stage, but the content and the related medium can be examined as well. Also, the involvement of the program coordinator can be explored, as an important piece in the process. In that case, if the mentoring program has a sounding board or other key stakeholders who oversee the coordinator, it is important that they get involved at this stage as much as they have been involved in the strategic aspects of the program.

The program needs to carefully examine the presence of all possible bottlenecks interfering with the well-functioning of the mentoring process. Once the feedback is collected, it needs to be analyzed properly so that proper actions are undertaken to modify the program as needed. Cloke and Goldsmith assert that: "*The assessment process needs to encourage lifelong learning, as a beginning rather than an end.*"

The above questions, if they are properly facilitated or posed, can bring about new insights for the ongoing refinement of the mentoring program and the mitigation of blind alleys. The question is then, how will they be exploited or utilized to that end? How will they be brought back to the system to ensure that it is functioning at its best? This is possible when those involved in the program are willing to assess what the roots or underlying assumptions behind unproductive behaviors are and see to correct them. This will take more than just acting on the findings, but will require determining the reason behind each action.

It is crucial that the outputs from those evaluation sessions be integrated back into the system in such a way that allows double-loop learning; which means that the underlying values of the unproductive behaviors are assessed and addressed accordingly instead of mere corrective actions being taken. When that happens, the mentoring program, in terms of process, gets better and better. Chris Argyris stated that: *"Two types of learning are necessary in all organizations. The first is single-loop learning: learning that corrects errors by changing routine behavior. The second is double-loop learning: learning that corrects errors by examining the underlying values and policies of the organization."*

It is as important for the program to change its course of action as it is to change the values that are supportive to the unproductive behavior. In practical terms the question can be formulated as thus: what factors are considered roadblocks to a more effective mentoring relationship? The program will make sure that when the factors are expressed, they are also examined to determine what values in the program allow them to emerge or perpetuate their existence. Some other feedback might imply that the program revise its selection criteria to foster more winning matches. Only then can real learning occur from review sessions or process monitoring. Still the program coordinator has to maintain close contact with the mentors and the mentees to supervise, coach and support them as the program's goals are met. Meanwhile, the program coordinator should not lose sight that the process needs to be assessed as well as the expected results.

2. Results evaluation

If the process evaluation is concerned with how the program is being implemented, the results evaluation is more concerned with the outputs, outcomes and impact of the program as planned; while process evaluation deals with activities, results evaluation deals with outcomes. They are, however, complementary as the results evaluation outlines the connection or linkages between the program activities and their results. This evaluation, called a summative evaluation, focuses on the changes that occurred in the personal and professional lives of the mentors and the mentees.

Unlike the process evaluation that needs to be conducted on a regular basis, the results evaluation is conducted at specific moments in time. It can be done when the program is half way through the implementation phase and just before graduation. If it wasn't for the process evaluation, the results evaluation would be considered much more as damage control. In terms of design, this evaluation can be simple or complex. It can be implemented via a questionnaire designed and administered to the participants of a program or to a population sample where control variables are monitored to ensure the accuracy of the results. In this context, two things are of great importance, the conducting of pre and post performance assessments and the establishment of results indicators.

As the participants enter the mentoring program it is crucial that through an application form, their profile or initial conditions be accurately assessed. This initial profiling will serve as a baseline which tells exactly how they are before joining the program. The baseline helps to determine the changes in the behaviors or in the competency development of the small business leaders. It initially requires a pre-assessment of which the results and findings will be compared to a post-assessment conducted at a later stage of the process. And these pre and post-assessments are the responsibility of the program coordinator. Once again, a questionnaire can be developed based on the program's mission and vision. In other words, based on the influence or impact the program wants to have on its participants, it needs to be able to monitor their progress and respond to that accordingly. At a specific moment in time, through the same questionnaire, the participants' statuses can be assessed after or during their participation in the program.

Some programs, according to the National Mentoring Partners have all interested or prospective mentees filling an application considered as the pre test questionnaire. Those who are not selected because of the program's admission capacity or other technical reasons apart from the eligibility criteria are on the program's waiting list. As such, at a later stage, they can be compared with those who have participated in the program. Since both groups hold the same characteristics, the results from the testing, positive or not, are worthy of attention.

Pre and post tests can indeed demonstrate the differences that a mentoring program had in the personal and professional lives of small business leaders considered as mentees. But to avoid biased results, there needs to be an investigation of other external factors or viable alternatives which can contribute to the influence as well. Therefore the introduction of control variables is a must. Grove and Huon recommended that the mentors be evaluated as well in terms of skills that they have developed after the training and orientation session and during the implementation of the mentoring relationship. This should help also in the refinement of the program from a mentor's perspective.

Edgcomb and Malm, arguing about the importance of well planned evaluation stated that: "*ultimately, the program needs to understand what the outcomes are and whether they are 'worth' the resource investment that the program is making in organizing and providing the service."* Thus, the program needs to agree on what the evaluation will focus on; in other terms, what will be evaluated and what will not be evaluated. And these questions are to be posed at the early stage of planning and designing or more specifically before the implementation phase. That is why the program needs to develop indicators which will assess its effectiveness in regards to the planned goals or expected results. In this context, a logic model can be an interesting tool to display the results or goals in relation to the activities based on specific indicators.

In fact, a logic model is well suited to address the breaking down of a vision into specific expected results monitored with key indicators. To facilitate this evaluation, a logic model with specific indicators for each output and outcome is of great importance. Kellogg Foundation, in support of this approach stated that: *"Using evaluation and the logic model results in effective programming and offers greater learning opportunities, better documentation of outcomes, and shared knowledge about what works and why."* As mentioned above, the evaluation's objective and process are not something which needs to be decided upon at the end of the program, but rather at its early conception. That is why the design of a mentoring program from a results-based logic model is a winning tool.

The tool is quite simple. It is a systematic view of what the program intends to achieve in time through specified activities with proper resources. And more importantly, it takes into account the indicators that will measure the effectiveness of the program according to the results achieved. The logic model is articulated around six key elements:

- the impact is the expression of the intended changes that happen at the organizational level partly because of the contribution of the program;
- the outcomes are the middle-term results, like changes in behavior, skills and competencies expected at the individual level because of a collection of different outputs;
- the outputs are the short term or direct results expected from each activity of the program;
- the activities are the process, tools, events and actions used in the program;
- the inputs are the resources infused into the program to undertake the activities;
- the enablers and constraints are the factors that influence the program in the specific context where the project is being implemented.

Sometimes programs are confused regarding the comprehension of impact, outcomes and outputs since they are all results. According to Cox and Luft, the difference between those various results lies in the amount of influence and control that the program may have regarding the results. The program has an important influence and control over the outputs (short term results) that derive from the activities, whereas, it has less control but only a certain influence over the outcomes (mid-term results) as they are one step removed from the activities which also allows external influence. In regards to the impact (long term results), it is considered as the vision of the program and is the results from the combination of various other factors beyond the scope of the program. That is the reason why it is recommended to use control variables when it comes to evaluating the outcomes and impact or the overall effectiveness of a program. A strategic mentoring program aimed at assisting small business leaders can be easily framed into a logic model (see appendix).

The logic model expresses that indicators are better tracked when they are directly related or connected to the expected results. The clearer the results, the better formulated will be the indicators. And both the (desired) end results and the indicators have to be determined at the outset. It was argued earlier that objectives/results have to be designed as "smart"; the same principles also apply to the indicators. It is important that the evaluation provides both quantitative and qualitative data and the indicators have to be designed for that purpose. The indicators will suggest the types and sources of information that needs to be collected. Since the purpose of the mentoring program is to accomplish a number of goals in the personal and organizational lives of the small business leaders it is important that these goals be assessed in due time. That will help in the promotion of strategic mentoring program as an effective tool to accompany small business leaders in their journey as they work at generating jobs and wealth to sustain the economy.

Overall, the evaluations have to be oriented toward learning opportunities or lessons that are likely to help the program improve the quality of its service and its effectiveness. As in the case of the process evaluation, the program should address the assumptions underlying each behavior in order to promote double-loop learning, the same remark applies to the context of the results evaluation. Evaluation sessions, whether they are conducted on a participatory manner, via data sampling or through other forms, are worthless if their outcomes are not transferred back into the program to ensure the existence of constant renewal, continual learning and adaptation. That is a necessary condition for the implementation of a successful strategic mentoring program.

A strategic mentoring program can therefore be considered as a vector of entrepreneurship development when it targets small business leaders. However, not all facilitated mentoring programs get to accomplish their objectives. It seems that the most effective ones follow a certain pattern when it comes to their design and implementation. The design is important because if it is not carefully planned; the program is not likely to meet its objectives.

In this context, it is recommended that a program starts by determining its reason for being (mission) as well as the changes (vision) it wants to see happen. In so doing, the program will be able to answer critical questions such as why should the program exist; whom will it serve; where will it be implemented and what will it seek to accomplish. The answers to those questions will help the program determine its mission and assess the type of changes it wants to bring about in the context of the small business leaders. In other words, it needs to develop a vision statement which should be effectively communicated and shared by its key stakeholders. The vision, from which specific goals will derive, is what will guide the path of the mentoring program and bring meaning to its activities.

Once the program is clear about what it intends to accomplish, the next step is to strategically and effectively target its participants, namely the mentees, the mentors and the program coordinator. The viability and effectiveness of the program largely depends on the strategic choices of mentors and mentees and the support that is provided to the mentors and mentees during the implementation phase of the program. Training and orientation sessions to the participants are a must throughout the implementation of the program to make sure that the relationships between the parties are properly nurtured. Finally, an environment has to be created where feedback is expressed and documented and the program needs to develop evaluation tools to ensure its continual refinement. All of this implies that effective facilitated mentoring programs do not just happen. Their success is more a matter of careful design, intentional planning and intelligent implementation than mere luck and this is exactly what this book wants to highlight.

Conclusion

Many economies of the world are counting on small businesses because of their recognized potential for job and wealth creation. Accordingly, any initiative which aims at upholding and enhancing the effectiveness of small business leaders is worth considering. However, it is to the benefit of the initiative to understand the reality that the small business is facing. These constraints, if not addressed, can indeed hinder their capacity to realize their potential. A small business development initiative has two responsibilities. First, assess the needs and challenges that the small business leaders face. Second assist them in developing skills, competencies and values that are conducive to personal development and organizational effectiveness in order to ensure profitability and responsibility in the marketplace.

Those skills and values can be best developed through experiential learning and role modeling. And, mentoring is one means by which real and enduring learning can occur. In fact, mentoring relationship involving experienced business leaders and leaders from start-up companies can facilitate the transfer of learning providing that it is well developed. Well developed implies that the mentoring program is strategically design and intelligently implemented. Such design and implementation require an effective targeting of the mentees, the mentors and the program coordinator; also an effective process based on developmental goals and proper action plan to meet the latter with monitoring and evaluation during all the various phases.

It is hoped that the design presented in this book helps decision-makers who consider strategic mentoring to be an important way to assist small business leaders to acquire leadership and management skills. Such skills are important for the success of their businesses and ultimately for job and wealth creation.

REFERENCES

Albrecht, C. 1994. *The North bound Train: Finding the Purpose, Setting the Direction, Shaping the Destiny of your Organization.* Amacom Publishing. New York, USA.

Allemann, E. 1991. *Managing Mentor Relationships in Organizations.* College Industry Education Proceedings. Leadership Development Consultants Inc. Mentor, Ohio. USA.

Allison M, Kaye J. 1997. *Strategic Planning for Non-Profit Organizations.* John Wiley & Sons Publishing. Canada.

Argyris, C. 1993. Education for Leading-Learning. *Organizational Dynamics Journal.* 21(3), 5-17.

Bauer T.N. 1999. Perceived Mentoring Fairness: Relationship with Gender, Mentoring Type, Mentoring Experience and Mentoring Needs, *Sex Roles* 40:211-25

Bauknight, N.D. Miller J.R. 2000. Fourth Party Logistics: The Evolution of Supply Chain outsourcing. *Harvard Business Review.*

Bennis, W. 1992. *On Becoming a Leader.* Addison Wesley Publishing. USA.

Bennis, W., Goldsmith, J. 2003. *Learning to Lead.* Basic Book Publishing. New York, USA.

Bloogood, Sapienza and Carsrud. 1995. Cited by Luthans F., Stajkovic A., Ibrayeva, E. 2000. Environmental and Psychological Challenges Facing Entrepreneurial Development in Transitional Economies. *Journal of World Business.* 35(1): 97-98

Buzzard S., Edgcomb, E. 2002. *Monitoring and Evaluation of Small Business Projects.* PACT, New York, USA.

Chrisman, J.J., & Leslie, J. 1989. Strategic, administrative, and operating problems: The impact of outsiders on small firm performance. *Entrepreneurship Theory & Practice*, 13 (30), 37-50

Cloke, K. Goldsmith, J. 2002. The End of Management and the Rise of Organizational Democracy. Jossey-Bass Publishing. California, USA.

Cloke, K. Goldsmith, J. 2003. *The Art of Waking People Up*. Jossey-Bass. USA.

Collins, J. 1997. *Built To Last: Success Habits of Visionary Companies*. Harper Business Publishing. New York, USA.

Collins, J. 2001. *Good to Great*. Harper Business Publishing. New York, USA.

Commission Recommendation concerning the Definition of Micro, Small and Medium-sized Enterprises. 2003. Notified under document number C (2003) 1422).

Conger, J. Benjamin, B. 1999. *Building Leaders*. Jossey-Bass Publishing. California, USA.

Cox, P. Luft, M. 2006. Managing for Change: Introducing the Art of Results Based Management. Plan Net Limited. Alberta, Canada.

Drucker, P. 2004. *The Daily Drucker*. Harper Business Publishing. New York, USA.

Edgecomb, E., Malm, E. 2002. Keep It Personalized: Consulting, Coaching and Mentoring for Microentrepreneurs. *FIELD Best Practice Guide* 4

Edwards, R. Usher, R. 2001. Lifelong Learning: A Post-Modern Condition of Education. *Adult Education Quarterly*. Vol. 51 no. 4 273-287.

Eisenhardt, K.M. 1989. Building theories from case study research. *Academy of Management Review*, 14, 4: 532-550.

Fahey, L. Randall, R. 1997. *MBA Stratégie, Les paramètres essentiels de la Gestion Stratégique dans une entreprise*. Editions Nouveaux Horizons. Paris, France.

Finkelstein, L.M, Allen T.D., Rhoton, L.A. An Examination of Role of Age in Mentoring Relationships. SAGE Publications. Group and Organizations Management, 28: 249-281.

Grove, J., Huon, G. 2003. *How to Implement a Peer Mentoring Program.* UNSW Academic Board. USA.

Handford, P. 2006. Research Study on Business Mentoring Activities. Report Affiliation of Multicultural and Social Services Agencies, Canada.

Harvard Business Essentials. 2004. *Coaching and Mentoring.* HPS Press Publishing. Massachusetts, USA.

Hersey, P. Blanchard, K. 1988. *Management of Organizational Behavior.* Prentice Hall Publishing. California, USA.

Holmes, S., Gibson, B. 2001. Definition of Small Business. Final Report. *The University of New Castle,* USA.

Kaplan, S. Be the Elephant. *Build a Bigger Business Better.* Workman Publishing. New York, USA.

Kellogg Foundation. 2004. Logic Model Development Guide. Michigan, USA.

Kotler, P. Dubois, B. 1997. *Marketing Management.* Editions Nouveaux Horizons. Paris, France.

Kotter, J. 1995. Leading Change. Pages 87-99 in Conger J.A., Spreitzer, G.M., Lawler III, E.E. 1999. *Leader's Change Handbook,* Jossey-Bass, Inc. New York, USA.

Kouses, J. Posner, B. 2003. *Credibility.* John Wiley & Sons Publishing. California, USA.

Luthans, F., Stajkovic, A.D. Ibrayera, E. 2000. Environmental and Psychological Challenges facing Entrepreneurial Development in Transitional Economies, *Journal of Word Business.* USA 35(1).

Makeower, J. 2000. *The Mentoring Handbook.* The National Environmental Education & Training Foundation. Washington, USA.

Maxwell, J. 2002. *Your Road map to success.* Thomas Nelson Publishing. Tenessee, USA.

Maxwell, J. 2004. *Winning with People*. Thomas Nelson Publishing. Tenessee, USA.

Maxwell, J. 2005. *The 360° Leader*. Thomas Nelson Publishing. California, USA.

Maxwell, J. Dorman, J. 1997. *Becoming a Person of Influence*. Thomas Nelson Publishing. Tenessee, USA.

Muchene, C. 2002. *Business Ethics. A Time to Change Our Behavior*. Price Waterhouse Coopers. Kenya.

Murray, M. 1991. *Beyond the Myths and Magic of Mentoring*. Josse-Bass, Inc. San Francisco, USA.

National Mentoring Partners. 2005. How to Build a Successful Mentoring Program. USA.

O'Neil, R.M, Sankowsky, D. 2001.The Caligula Phenomenon. Mentoring Relationships and Theoretical Abuse. *Journal of Management Inquiry*, 10:206-216.

Perkins, D.N.T. 2003. *Leadership Sous 0°*. Editions du Trésor Caché. Québec, Canada.

President Bush Discusses Economy, Small Business in Alabama. http://www.whitehouse.gov/news/releases/2003/11/200 31103-7.html visited on January 8, 2007.

Roberts, A. 1999. Homer's Mentor: Duties Fulfilled or Misconstrued? *History of Education Journal*. London, UK. Accessed on the Internet *http://home.att.net* on 26/03/07.

Shea, F.G. 1997. *Mentoring: A Practical Guide*. Crisp Publications, USA.

Sinetar, S. 1998. The Mentor's Spirit. St. Martin's Griffin Edition. New York, USA.

Thierry Graduate School of Leadership. About Vision, in KA *Mastery of Change*, of Lesly Jules, 2006, Brexgata Clearing House o.b.o. the faculty of the Thierry Graduate School of leadership.

Thierry Graduate School of Leadership. Corporate Social Responsibility. What is it really?, in KA *Avenues of Thought in*

Ethics, of Lesly Jules, 2006, Brexgata Clearing House o.b.o. the faculty of the Thierry Graduate School of leadership.

Thierry Graduate School of Leadership. Lonely Leaders, in KA *On Leaders and Followers I & II*, of Lesly Jules, 2006, Brexgata Clearing House o.b.o. the faculty of the Thierry Graduate School of leadership.

Thierry Graduate School of Leadership. Reading: "The Odyssey" by Homer, in KA *Leaders and Followers*, of Lesly Jules, 2005, Brexgata Clearing House o.b.o. the faculty of the Thierry Graduate School of leadership.

Thierry Graduate School of Leadership. Reading: On Knowing Human Nature and Behavior, in KA *Human Nature and Behavior*, of Lesly Jules, 2005, Brexgata Clearing House o.b.o. the faculty of the Thierry Graduate School of leadership.

Vesper, K.H. 1990. *New Venture Strategies* (revised ed.). Englewood Cliffs, NJ: Prentice Hall.

Welch, J. 2005. *Winning.* Harper Business Publishing. New York, USA.

APPENDIX

SITUATION: Small businesses are reputed for job and wealth creation. However, this potential is not always realized due to a lack of management and entrepreneurial skills faced by small business leaders. Those skills are better developed through experiential learning. And strategic mentoring is an effective means that leads there. Therefore, this program aims at providing mentoring opportunities to 20 small business leaders as for the first year of the program's existence.			ORGANIZATION: Centre Spécialisé de Leadership (CSL) PROGRAM TIMEFRAME : 3 years	
	HOW?	WHAT WE WANT?		WHY?
INPUTS	ACTIVITIES	OUTPUTS	OUTCOMES	IMPACT
Mentors	Advertise the program to prospective mentors and mentees	15 mentor applications are received and 25 mentee's.		
Mentees	Screen applications and organize orientation session about the program to mentors and mentees.	10 mentors and 15 mentees are retained for the program.		
Staff with management and leadership skills	Facilitate training sessions for mentors and mentees.	The selected mentors and mentees understand how the program works and are ready to start meeting.	The mentors have been significantly influenced by the program. They want to stay longer in the program.	The economy benefits from profitable businesses that create more wealth and jobs.
Facility	Supervise and provide support to the mentoring relationships.	The mentoring relationship is doing well as the participants develop learning plans. They are meeting on a regular basis and give feedback to the program.	The mentees have proven management, leadership and entrepreneurial skills which transferred in the context of their business, make them more profitable.	
Training materials	Host recognition sessions with mentors, mentees along with other key stakeholders and publish the milestones in newsletters and other mediums.	The mentors are satisfied with the program. The mentees are graduated. Other mentors join the program.	The graduated mentees volunteer to serve as mentors in the program.	
Promotional materials				
Financial support				
INDICATORS				
		Outputs	Outcomes	Long Term Outcomes (Impact)
		- Number of mentors and mentees planned (…) vs. realized (…) - Number of matches planned (…) vs. realized (…) - Number of mentoring sessions or hours planned (…) vs. realized (…) - Number of satisfied mentors and graduated mentees planned (…) vs. realized (…)	- Change in the mentors' perception regarding mentoring. - Coached employees understand the vision of the company and are more motivated to contribute - Customers are satisfied. - Significant increase in the return of the companies. - Number of mentors retained and number of mentees who become coaches.	Change in the economy as a result of the job and wealth creation.

Logic Model of a Strategic Mentoring Program

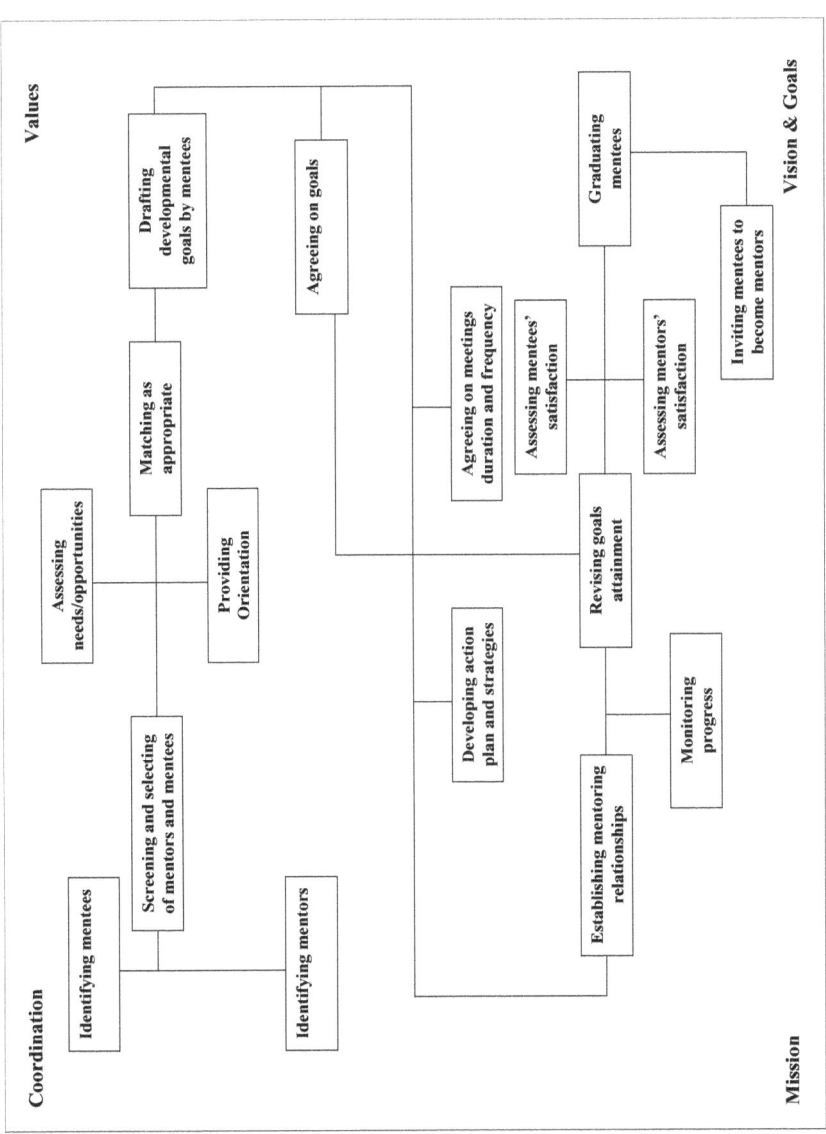